How to Get the Most Out of Philosophy

Third Edition

Douglas J. Soccio
Shasta College

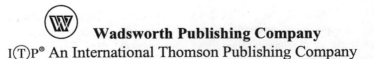

Wadsworth Publishing Company
I(T)P® An International Thomson Publishing Company

Belmont, CA • Albany, NY • Bonn • Boston • Cincinnati
Detroit • Johannesburg • London • Madrid • Melbourne • Mexico City
New York • Paris • Singapore • Tokyo • Toronto • Washington

For students everywhere—
but especially for first-generation students
and their families

This is your education. Customize it. Work at it. By enrolling in college, you are accepting a personal invitation to participate in a "great conversation." Plato characterized his teacher, the philosopher Socrates, as a guide who helped others climb out of the cave of ignorance. But Socrates, one of the greatest teachers of all time, always insisted that the teacher only "draws wisdom" out of the pupil, and only the pupil can provide the will.

In the spirit of Socrates, I hope this book helps you on your own journey "out of the cave."

Contents

Preface to Instructors
(and Curious Students)

I am regularly amazed at the seemingly "obvious" things many of my students don't know at all, or fail to recognize the importance of. Things like studying the course syllabus—and keeping it for the entire term. Things like carefully following formatting instructions for writing assignments. Things like bringing the textbook to class. Things like using the glossary and index. Things like coming by during scheduled office hours and asking questions.

When the first edition of *How to Get the Most Out of Philosophy* came out bundled with *Archetypes of Wisdom*, it generated two kinds of responses. I was both surprised and gratified by the intensity of positive interest. Instructors *and students* requested additional, stand-alone copies, which, alas, were not available at that time.

Interestingly, the first edition also provoked a more troubling kind of reaction. Some *philosophy instructors* (not students) trivialized the book as "hokey," "simplistic," and "belaboring the obvious." As I said in the preface to the second edition, I trust that this other reaction came from instructors whose undergraduate students arrive having completed four years of sophisticated college prep courses in high school. Perhaps many of the more disdainful instructors were themselves good students from highly stable backgrounds, and so remain unaware of the kinds of things many promising students simply haven't learned in high school. But the success of the second edition has confirmed my belief that many of us (students and professors) begin college ignorant of the very practices, expectations, and cultural norms that seem so "obvious" once they're identified and internalized.

Indeed, the second edition proved even more successful than the first, as students and philosophy professors recommended this "handbook of student wisdom" to friends, relatives, counselors and others, not just philosophy students and philosophy teachers. This expanded third edition has been revised in light of the helpful suggestions so many kind students, professors, and others have shared with me. I am particularly grateful to my own students for their interest and help in my efforts to identify more of the "taken for granteds" that even the most conscientious college professors can overlook because, ironically, they seem so "obvious."

As college becomes accessible to more people, today's diverse student body will include ever-increasing numbers of first-generation students, students trying to juggle family responsibilities, jobs, and solid course loads, students from shaky environments, and students who did "well enough" in high school, but still arrive in college a bit naive, disorganized, marginally motivated, and, unsurprisingly, even a little insecure. This book is for such students— and for the instructors who want to help them succeed, not just in class, but in college and beyond.

As a first-generation college student, I know first-hand the consequences of "not knowing the ropes." Because I was a "bright" high school student, my teachers and family just assumed that I'd probably go to college—so I assumed it, too. Lacking any more precise plans than "going to college," and trying to save money, I began my college education by driving across town to the closest community college. I never thought one way or the other about the long-term effects of going to a community college as opposed to a big-name college or university. I just vaguely thought that some people "went to college" and then went out and asked for—and got—jobs based on the fact that people who "went to college" became "successful." All of this was very general, however, and so I selected a "general education" major. I had vague goals, but no focus.

When I was ready to transfer to the local state university for upper division courses, I approached a couple of my favorite instructors for letters of recommendation. I figured that since I got good grades, and since I liked them and learned a lot from them, my instructors would be happy to recommend me to a four-year college. I was wrong—at least initially. Each professor politely informed me that he knew nothing about me. I had never been by their offices, and I had only taken one course from each of them. Eventually, they must have taken pity on me, because after checking my transcript and chatting with me a while about my plans, each wrote me a generic letter of recommendation.

In hindsight, I understand that, as a young man, I brought a certain working-class ethic with me to college. One tenet of that ethic is that a person does not use flattery to get ahead: You stand or fall on the quality of your performance, your work. I mistakenly viewed asking my teachers for help outside of class, or just talking with them about their classes, as flattery. Consequently, I had deliberately avoided going by to see my professors. I was so worried about being perceived as a flatterer, rather than a hard worker, that I deliberately avoided my teachers out of class.

Although I had plenty of love and support from my family, I had no one to teach me about things like letters of recommendation, or how to relate to a PROFESSOR. None of us knew much about college—to say nothing of philosophy courses.

My point here is not to tell stories about myself, but to suggest how easy it easy to lose sight of the complexity of the day-to-day factors that bear on student success or failure. The philosophy instructors who reacted negatively to the first edition may have devoted so much of their attention to the subject matter at hand, that they overlooked some of these complicating factors. The fact is, however, that the great variety of students coming to us to learn philosophy only intensifies the need for books like *How to Get the Most Out of Philosophy*, Third Edition.

We must not assume that most of our students will have graduated from high school with solid reading, writing and thinking skills. In some parts of the country, it is still possible to graduate from high school without ever writing an argument paper or analytic essay. Consider, for just one example, the case of a student I had this past semester in a critical thinking and writing course. At my college, the students who take this course must meet an English composition prerequisite. They also tend to be focused and highly motivated. In short, they are among our best students. After weeks of frustration and tension, one of my students, the daughter of a high school English teacher, finally told me that in four years of high school, she had *never* had to write analytically. Worse yet, she was not used to having the logic and sense of her writing evaluated. Having taught the critical thinking and writing course for some time, I can verify that this young woman was not alone, and probably—sadly—was not exaggerating. I have been told about, and educational literature confirms, countless similar cases.

Anecdotal literature and group projects (collaborative learning) are quite the thing right now, and one consequence is that many students have been required to write only journals and expressive essays, to "present" class projects orally or visually, and to read expressive—not argumentative—literature. And, of course, the widespread "opening up" of the notion of critical thinking means that just because our students have done something called "critical thinking," we cannot assume that whatever they've learned bears any close resemblance to what philosophers mean by that term. Your philosophy course may very well be the first sustained exposure to thinking and writing critically about critical literature that some of your students have ever had.

How to Get the Most Out of Philosophy, Third Edition is not intended to compensate for truly remedial skills, nor can its basic advice overcome a truly unstable life circumstance. But maybe it can be just enough of a boost to make a difference between success or failure. Sometimes the smallest help can make a difference.

No matter what kind of philosophy course you teach, no matter where you teach, you are likely to have some students who will benefit from the kind of advice and encouragement it is easy to forget to give—because it seems so obvious to those of us who have been in school nearly all of our lives. It does us wizened old profs—and our students—good to remember that "'twas not always so."

New to the Third Edition

Users of the second edition of *How to Get the Most Out of Philosophy* will note that the third edition has been expanded and reorganized. Changes include:

- New material on self-respect (which is distinguished from self-esteem).

- An improved, simplified MLA-based style guide, with more citation examples.

- A brief discussion of online and Internet citations and sources, focusing on the need for critical scrutiny.

- New material has been added to the Beginning Philosopher's Bibliography, including a few philosophy websites and online resources, and the writing style guides have been updated.

- The entire text has been updated and polished. New boxed tips and quotes are both useful and enriching.

How to Get the Most Out of Philosophy On the World Wide Web

The Wadsworth Philosophy Shoppe is a nifty website provided by Wadsworth Publishing Company, the publisher of this book. *The Wadsworth Philosophy Shoppe* has all sorts of information about their publications (as you might expect). What you might not expect, however, is that many of their authors, practicing philosophers with differing interests and styles, post interesting information there, too. This website is a great opportunity to browse in a specialized "virtual bookstore" and to communicate with philosophers from around the world. (For more information about online philosophy, see the Beginning Philosopher's Bibliography at the end of the book.)

As this book is going to press, I am just beginning to work on home pages for the third editions of *How to Get the Most Out of Philosophy* and *Archetypes of Wisdom*. Once up and running, I look forward to hearing from you. I like to think that my philosophy books are realistically helpful and encouraging, and any insight or advice you choose to share will be gratefully received and seriously considered. Wadsworth's philosophy website address is: http://philosophy.wadsworth.com

INTRODUCTION

What To Expect

If we do only what is required of us we are slaves, the moment we do more we are free.

Cicero

Have you ever pondered the "big questions"? What's the meaning of life? Is there really a God? If God exists, why does the world seems so crazy? What's wrong with just living for myself? Is everything just a matter of opinion? What is justice? Maybe everything's a big illusion, some kind of dream?

If you're like almost everybody, you have what I think of as a *philosophical impulse,* a natural curiosity about fundamental questions. Most people seem to respond to this philosophical impulse without prompting. High school and college students sometimes refer to informal philosophical pondering as "bull sessions," and sometimes they are—but not always. Something else may also be going on, something triggered by what Plato and Aristotle (two philosophical megastars) called the *sense of wonder.*

You're possibly wondering what your philosophy course will be like. It won't be another "bull session." Philosophy courses are related to the philosophical impulse in much the same way that joining the school soccer team is related to playing soccer at a picnic with your friends. It's the same game, but the commitment to conditioning and fundamentals, to a schedule set by someone else, and the need to accept the evaluations of an impartial, specially trained referee, can make it feel as if they are really two completely different games.

Succeeding in a philosophy class requires a willingness to think in a structured, critical way at scheduled times, whether or not you are in a pondering mood—just like being a member of the soccer team requires you to practice or play at scheduled times, whether or not you are in the "soccering" mood. Your coach may put you in as the goalie, when you prefer to play forward—just like your philosophy instructor may want you to think and write about the existence of God, when you would rather think and write about the pursuit of pleasure. One of the great sources of student misinformation is the notion that to think carefully you must be "in the mood." As you'll discover, if you don't know already, thinking is more like physical exertion than we sometimes want to admit. You'll discover that you have the ability to think carefully—just like you have the ability to run wind sprints—whether or not you're in the mood.

One key to success in philosophy class is to begin the term with a firm resolve to participate, whether or not you are "in the mood." When your interest wanes, remind yourself that you have the ability to direct your mind just as you have the ability to pump those jelly legs for the umpteenth wind sprint. Most of the frustrations students have with philosophy courses can be overcome, or at least reduced to annoyances.

This handbook will help you make the most of your philosophy course (and your other courses, as well) by providing useful information and tips about the basic elements that affect your experience in any college course: the subject, the text, the instructor, and your own resolve and circumstances.

Although you cannot do anything *directly* about the subject itself, your teacher, or which text your instructor assigns, you can exert considerable *influence* on yourself, and some *influence* on your instructor.

How to Get the Most Out of Philosophy, Third Edition, is based on articles and books about teaching, on conversations with professors at community colleges, private liberal arts colleges, state universities, and world-famous research universities. Most of all, it is based on my interactions with thousands of students of almost every conceivable background and ability.

Some of the information that follows may be new to you, and some of it will be the same old stuff you've heard most of your life. The point of hearing it again is what the nineteenth-century Danish philosopher **Søren Kierkegaard (1813-1855)** called *edification*, a lesson that *changes us* for the better. Sometimes, we can be encouraged and motivated when someone else says what we already know.

I have made explanations and examples deliberately brief so that you can quickly scan the entire book, and then return to pertinent sections as often as you need to. Everything that follows is designed to help you study efficiently, to take advantage of the accumulated wisdom of philosophy students and instructors, to avoid unnecessary anxiety, to get satisfactory grades, and to learn something of value. When the same advice occurs in more than one place, it's there to make it easier for you to review individual sections (say, just the section on essay tests) with assurance that all the basics are there.

You can read *How to Get the Most Out of Philosophy*, Third Edition relatively quickly, and I highly recommend reading it straight through right away. Doing so will get you fired up about philosophy, about your education, about yourself. Then, you can dip into various sections as needed, for encouragement, advice, or reminders.

I hope you find philosophy as valuable and interesting as I did when I was a freshman. Please accept this book as part of my way of saying thank you to all of my teachers, so many of whom have been my students.

PART ONE

Philosophy Courses

I do not know how to teach philosophy without becoming a disturber of the peace.

> *Baruch Spinoza*

If you've never had a philosophy course, you're probably curious about what you're getting into. Most college students have had science courses, history classes, English courses, and social science classes in high school. But for most undergraduates, philosophy is new territory.

Chapter 1 discusses special features of philosophy courses, and offers suggestions that can help you avoid some of the more common anxieties and pitfalls that can slow down beginning philosophy students. Chapter 2 alerts you to important features of philosophical writing.

CHAPTER 1

How To Survive
A Philosophy Class

The real reason for failure is unwillingness, the pretended reason, inability.

Seneca

Most philosophy courses focus on extended arguments used to justify value judgments and truth claims, the search for very basic principles, standards of meaning and knowledge, and so forth. As a general rule, philosophical questions cannot be settled by the empirical sciences or appeals to religious faith—though scientific evidence and religious beliefs do play a role in some philosophical speculation. Philosophical questions cannot be settled by simple appeals to personal conviction and experience, or by referring to psychological or social causes—although they, too, play a role in philosophical thinking.

Regardless of the specific format or content of your introductory philosophy courses, you will be encouraged to think for yourself in a critical and sophisticated way, to recreate others' arguments fairly and accurately, and to provide reasons for any position you take on philosophical topics.

The following passage from **René Descartes' (1596-1650)** *Rules for the Direction of the Mind* reminds us that our beliefs remain shaky and "second hand," not really ours, until we think them through for ourselves:

Further, supposing now that all were wholly open
and candid, and never thrust upon us doubtful positions as true, but expounded every matter in good
faith, yet since scarce anything has been asserted
by any one man the contrary of which has not been
alleged by another, we should be eternally uncer-
tain which of the two to believe. It would be no use
to total up the testimonies in favour of each, meaning to follow that opinion which is supported by
the greater number of authors; for if it is a question
of difficulty that is in dispute, it is more likely
that the truth would have been discovered by few
than by many. But even though all these men
agreed among themselves, what they teach would
not suffice for us. For we shall not, e.g., turn out to
be mathematicians though we know by heart all
the proofs others have elaborated, unless we have
an intellectual talent that fits us to resolve difficulties of any kind. Neither, though we may have
mastered all the arguments of Plato and Aristotle,
if yet we have not the capacity for passing solid
judgment on these matters, shall we become Philosophers; we should have acquired the knowledge
not of a [philosophy], but of history.

Philosophy instructors want to help you acquire philosophical *understanding, not just information or empty technique.* They are as
interested in your learning to ask the right questions as they are in
helping you get the right answers. You will not be expected to
"solve" or "settle" great philosophical issues, only to understand
some basic ones, and to think carefully about them.

Because philosophers themselves disagree about the proper
way to philosophize, there are no universally accepted formulae
to follow in philosophy courses like there are in math or science
courses. Your philosophy instructor may disagree with many
things in this book—for carefully thought-out reasons. If your
school has more than one introductory philosophy teacher, it
won't be surprising to find that different teachers have different
approaches to the "same course." The next time you're in the bookstore, take a look at the texts used in different sections of the same

course. They will give you some idea of how much variety there can be in one philosophy department.

Most likely, however, all of the introductory philosophy courses will share a fundamental interest in critical thinking and writing, the importance of supporting claims with reasons, and a commitment to encouraging you to think for yourself. A philosophy class is not the place to be if you are intellectually lazy, or lack curiosity, because you will be required to respond to philosophers' arguments in a rational way.

The influential eighteenth century philosopher **Immanuel Kant (1724-1804)** used the term "self-imposed tutelage" to characterize a kind of mental laziness that sometimes makes thinking for ourselves difficult. Tutelage is a form of slavery or dependency. Kant thought that the process of thinking for ourselves could release us from "self-imposed tutelage." He wrote:

> Tutelage is the inability to use one's natural powers without direction from another. This tutelage is called "self-imposed" because it came about not by any absence of rational competence but simply a lack of courage and resolution to use one's reason without direction from another. *Sapere aude!*— Dare to reason! Have the courage to use your own minds!—is the motto of the enlightenment.
>
> Laziness and cowardice explain why so many . . . remain under a life-long tutelage and why it is so easy for some . . . to set themselves up as the guardians of all the rest. . . . If I have a book which understands for me, a pastor who has a conscience for me, a doctor who decides my diet, I need not trouble myself. If I am willing to pay, I need not think. Others will do it for me.

Your philosophy instructor will almost certainly be an enemy of "self-imposed tutelage."

Philosophy instructors vary in the emphasis they put on factual and historical information, but as a rule, philosophy courses do not require learning as many names and dates as a history course might, or many facts and technical terms the way a geography course can—though you cannot critically consider an issue if you do not memorize some basic information, whether it be historical, technical, or the meanings of key terms and concepts. Just because philosophy courses don't usually involve extensive concentration on facts does not mean that you can slough off learning and memorizing key facts, figures, terms, concepts, and their contexts.

Charles "Gus" Garrigus, a lifelong educator and former poet laureate of California, says that "Memorization provides furniture for the mind." Garrigus argues, rightly I believe, that rote memorization has been getting a bad rap in educational circles for some time. And, certainly, *mere* memorization cannot substitute for more refined abilities: comprehension, assessment, speculation, and the like. But, as Garrigus says, it is impossible just to "think" without thinking *about something*. We must furnish our minds with facts, names, dates, terms, definitions, arguments, principles, standards. The welder needs to *learn and memorize* safety procedures, metallurgic properties, and such, and, certainly, you expect to memorize facts and terms in biology and Spanish classes. So, too, plan to memorize technical philosophical terms, figures, and, where relevant, historical context.

Academic excellence begins with a solid foundation of information for each subject you study, beginning with terminology, progressing from information to concepts and practices, culminating in rational evaluation and critically creative thinking.

ACQUIRING INFORMED OPINIONS

You cannot judge by annoyance.	*Idries Shah*

Although you probably already have opinions about many of the topics covered in philosophy courses, you probably have not had the opportunity to analyze and justify these opinions in the sustained, critical way that's common to most philosophy classes. One of the things you can expect to study in a philosophy course is the difference between *uninformed opinion* (often called "mere opinion") and *informed opinion*.

A common misconception about philosophy is that it's "just one philosopher's opinion versus another philosopher's opinion." This idea rests on a fundamental confusion about different levels of justification. **"Mere" belief** *is the conviction that something is true based solely on the sincere conviction of the believer that it is true.* A tiny—inadequate—step up from mere belief is **uninformed opinion,** *conviction based on vague notions, common prejudices, and a variety of inexpert sources such as the mass media and individuals speaking out on issues that they have not subjected to sustained, organized, careful, critical, scrutinized study.*

Sadly, today's cultural climate seems pretty hostile to informed, critical opinion. Informed, critical opinion doesn't make good "sound bites" on the evening news, nor is it compatible with blind allegiance to a political party, social doctrine, or any strong belief. Television talk shows inundate us with shouting, belligerent, "sincere" advocates for all sorts of beliefs. What they rarely present—or even tolerate—is the time and care necessary for thoughtful reflection and analysis of these often very important issues. Certainly, most advertisers, and many politicians and social reformers, don't want you to think for yourself—they want your agreement, allegiance, or financial support.

Your philosophy instructor will help you develop some thinking skills that can free you from self-imposed, media-imposed, even friends-and-family imposed tutelage. Thinking for yourself is like accomplishing some task for yourself—it's more difficult than letting someone else do it, but it's also much more satisfying to be able to do things for yourself. It's psychologically satisfying because skills mastery is intrinsically pleasing, and it's liberating in the practical realm because you are in the driver's seat when you think for yourself.

Expect your instructor to demand that you *present reasons* to support your opinions with rigor and clarity. Don't despair. She or he is there to teach you how to meet a higher standard of proof, not to show up your faults or cut you down. The only way to learn how to present good reasons is by recognizing bad—or nonexistent—ones, especially when they're your own.

Fear of error is probably second only to willed ignorance as a stumbling block to learning. That's too bad, because an error that is acknowledged is no longer an error.

A common method of teaching philosophy involves deliberately challenging your present beliefs—not because they are necessarily insupportable, but also to help you see just how sound they are. It can be quite discouraging to discover that you can't support some of your most cherished beliefs. It can also be quite exciting to discover that you can. In either case, your instructor is likely to be more concerned with helping you learn *how* to think philosophically than with teaching you *what* to think. This kind of teaching can be initially frustrating if you're used to being told "the truth" by authority figures. But once you experience the intellectual excitement of challenging important ideas, "deliberate philosophical tension" will become quite stimulating.

> In one way or another, virtually all of the world's wisdom traditions teach that, for most of us, wisdom does not come without some struggle and disappointment. Learning to learn is no exception. There is no "painless" way to become a good student—but, then, there is no painless way to become a good child, or parent, or athlete, or friend.

The combination of sometimes controversial, often abstract topics, and the introduction of new standards of proof can confuse new philosophy students. Stick with it. Work at refining your thinking skills, and initial frustration will turn to interest and possibly even enchantment. You'll take justifiable pride in your more polished thinking.

SPECIAL FEATURES OF PHILOSOPHY COURSES

• Philosophy courses devote considerable attention to reasons and arguments. Precision and clarity are highly valued.

• Students—and instructors—are expected to defend interpretations and positions rationally.

• Many philosophical arguments are complex and abstract.

• There are often equally compelling reasons supporting conflicting points of view.

• The topics studied in philosophy courses often challenge or directly reject commonly held opinions.

• Philosophy instructors often place as much (if not more) emphasis on the reasoning offered for a position as they do on "getting the right answer."

• Many (if not most) of the philosophies covered will seem persuasive and flawed at the same time. (That's because they are.)

• Philosophy has been characterized as the art of questioning. Philosophy courses can be frustrating to students used to getting "the correct answer."

• No philosophical idea or value is sacred. Any philosophical position worth holding is a fair subject for critical analysis.

GETTING THE MOST OUT OF A PHILOSOPHY (OR ANY) CLASS

• **Develop a mature attitude.** Give all ideas a fair initial hearing, even if you can't imagine holding them yourself. Don't "shoot from the hip" and make impulsive, uninformed prejudgments.

• **Participate in class.** Volunteer to answer questions when the instructor asks them. Offer supporting examples. Ask for clarification.

• **Don't confuse having a strong opinion with being right.** You probably hold strong beliefs about many issues you've not recently (if ever) thoroughly and objectively investigated.

• **Don't immediately raise your objections to new ideas.** Make sure you understand the *entire* issue and its significance to the point being developed in class before raising objections. If you find yourself *repeatedly* tempted to object to "wrong" beliefs, you may be locked into a defensive attitude that will prevent you from understanding many of the things you are expected to learn. Don't try to get a good education (especially a philosophical one) and also hold onto all of your present ideas. *You won't have gotten much of an education if you are the same person at graduation as you were when you began college.*

• **Practice the principle of charity.** In simple terms, the principle of charity directs you to begin your analysis of a passage or argument by interpreting any ambiguities and apparent inconsistencies to the advantage of the point being advanced. This will prevent you from reading with a selective bias or prejudice against a position that challenges a cherished belief, or that expresses a new idea. Your first careful reading of a philosophical passage should always be based on the assumption that the author's intention is to present good reasons for his or her position—and that he or she is capable of doing so. This attitude gives you the best chance of understanding the original argument. It minimizes the chances that you will distort ideas that you don't like. Psychologists who study learning report that people have the most difficulty understanding and remembering ideas they disagree with. That's not surprising. But you can use that information to help you become a better student and better thinker by consciously resisting the impulse to look for weaknesses before you fully grasp a position. (CAUTION: DO NOT EXPECT YOUR PROFESSOR TO READ YOUR WORK UNDER THE PRINCIPLE OF CHARITY. IN ORDER TO STRENGTHEN YOUR WRITING AND THINKING SKILLS, YOUR INSTRUCTOR WILL PROBABLY INTERPRET GAPS, INCONSISTENCIES, AND AMBIGUITIES AS ERRORS ON YOUR PART. ALWAYS HOLD YOURSELF TO A HIGH STANDARD OF EXPRESSION AND PROOF, JUST TO BE SAFE.)

• **Think in terms of understanding rather than judging.** Reread the preceding material.

• **Continually ask yourself *why* you believe X and not Y.**

• **Don't settle for superficial, easy answers.**

• **Work, work, work.** Accept the fact that to understand what's going on in class you'll need to read your assignments on time, and most likely need to reread them once or twice.

• **Read, read, and reread.** There is no substitute for carefully reading all assignments. The more you read, the better you read and the more you learn.

• **Come to class with questions and ask them.**

• **If a point made in class is unclear, wait a few minutes to see if subsequent remarks clear it up. If not, ask for clarification.** If you cannot bring yourself to ask questions during class, make a specific note of your confusion. After class, write your question neatly, and give it to your instructor before the next class meeting. Meanwhile, study the issue on your own, and, if necessary, modify your notes.

• **Ask for clarification of all assignments when they are made.** Don't *ever* leave class without being very sure you understand all assignments.

• **Follow instructions.** Don't make *any modification* without *specific—explicit—permission from your instructor.*

• **Exchange phone numbers with at least one other class member, and agree to share notes and information when one of you has missed a class.** (To abuse this agreement is to risk destroying it.)

• **Always take your book to class.** You never know when it will come in handy.

• **Sit up front, toward the center.** Studies indicate that where you sit can affect your performance in class. If you sit near the instructor, you'll feel more involved in class. It's more difficult to daydream and doze off right under the professor's nose. From a statistical point of view, the most academically dangerous seats are those that create a sense of distance and anonymity—far back, rear sides, the obscure middle of large lecture halls, and so forth.

You'll be much more confident about asking questions if you come to class prepared. It's undertandably difficult to ask questions if you're not sure what's in the reading assignment. Writing down a question often triggers the answer to it, or clarifies the problem in a way that indicates what's needed to get an answer.

DECIDING WHAT IS NOTE-WORTHY

• **Always come to class prepared to take notes.** You'll certainly want to note important due dates, changes in the assignment schedule, and so forth, in addition to lecture notes.

• **Be spacious.** Take plenty of paper to class so that you can allow plenty of space between key words and phrases in your notes. If you use lined paper, skip two or three lines between each distinct idea, argument, issue, term, and so forth. When you review your notes, you can add clarifying details from the textbook, dictionaries, study sessions with other students. You may find it helpful to make two columns for notes, one for basic lecture information, and the other to be used when adding clarifying details *later*.

• **Gear your notes to your instructor's teaching style as follows:**

> **Lectures that repeat the text.** Some instructors prefer to follow the text closely in their lectures. In that case, you won't need to take very thorough notes regarding the *information* conveyed in class. You'll probably do best by *not* trying to write down every name, date, definition, and idea mentioned in class (you can look them up in the text). Instead, listen carefully for new insights or alternative explanations of complex ideas. Make note of them— use key phrases that will remind you of examples, analogies, or simplified definitions when you review and flesh out your notes later (as you, of course, will do).

Lectures that convey information not found in text. If your instructor's lectures contain a wealth of new information, you will need to take careful, thorough notes. You might consider developing your own form of shorthand. If you do, be consistent. For example, many people use w/ to mean "with" and @ to mean "according to," and so forth.

Lectures that consist of wide-ranging elaborations on key ideas, but do not repeat or strictly follow the text. Don't attempt to record such lectures verbatim, and don't attempt to organize their content as you take notes. Some of the best lecturers are the most difficult to take notes from because their lectures have a life of their own. No two lectures on Socrates, for instance, are ever the same for some spell-binding master-lecturers. Don't be frustrated. Relax and "go with the flow." Listen actively. Respond spontaneously with your own inner dialogue. Record useful bits and pieces from your reactions, using key phrases. You cannot (and need not) take exhaustive, conventional notes from some lecturers. In most cases of this nature, the purpose of the lecture is to involve you in the *philosophical process* (called "doing philosophy"). Your instructor probably expects you to get detailed information from the text. Such "demonstration" lectures expose you to philosophy in practice. They are designed to inspire you, not to duplicate the text.

• **Record all new and/or complex information and ideas.** Don't assume that you'll be able to remember everything you hear in class. There may simply be too many new ideas for that to be possible. Further, you will need time to distill new ideas. Take notes that will enable you to concentrate on relationships and connections among ideas. Copy all alternative definitions and explanations for technical philosophical terms. Record illustrative examples.

- **Don't try to take notes word-for-word.** Jot down key words and phrases, make diagrams.

- **Record *all* charts, definitions, and outlines from the board or overhead projections (if they are not from the text).**

- **Take special care to RECORD EVERY IDEA YOU DISLIKE.** Cognitive scientists have shown that we tend to overlook, forget, or distort ideas that challenge or seriously disagree with our most cherished desires and fundamental beliefs. We tend to trivialize and unconsciously alter opposing ideas to make them less threatening. Unpleasant and threatening ideas are also more difficult to understand, so you'll need to put special effort into recording them accurately and completely—and into studying them later.

- **Be very careful to include *all* modifiers and qualifying terms.** Words like "always," "sometimes," "probably," "might," "never," and the like, are crucial parts of claims. Leaving them out significantly changes the meaning of the original idea. Example: Changing "Philosophy and religion sometimes overlap" to "Philosophy and religion overlap" alters the meaning of the original sentence.

- **Ask questions and make comments as part of your notes.** Keep track of any questions (or strong reactions) you have to ideas expressed in class. Use a "?" to mean "why?" Be brief but clear. "Proof?" can mean "How does X know? What's the evidence?" "!" can mean "great!" or "wow!" Use "N" for "no" and "Y" for yes to indicate disagreement or agreement. Use "NB" from the Latin *nota bene* for "note well" (pay attention).

- **Polish your notes soon after you take them.** Go over your notes the same day you make them. Try to make a quick polish within an hour or so after you've taken your notes. Fill in details. Restate cloudy passages. Use the generous spaces you left to amplify your necessarily incomplete notes.

> Don't reduce your instructor to a talking textbook. You have a textbook to use as a textbook. Think of your instructor as a valuable source of enrichment, clarification, guidance, and support. To get the most out class, don't treat class time as study hall and don't treat lectures as substitutes for careful reading.

WHY ATTENDANCE MATTERS

• **Studying philosophy is a skill and a way of thinking, in addition to being a set of key issues and individuals.** You need to experience the way your instructor "does philosophy" on a regular basis if you want to do more than just acquire philosophical information.

• **You're more likely to learn if you feel safe and comfortable, and you're more likely to feel safe and comfortable if you know what's going on.** Instructors often modify schedules, announce extensions for assignments, and so forth, in class. You want to get this useful information right away.

• **Getting to know and recognize classmates, no matter how casually, will enhance your sense of belonging.** You'll be more able to discuss course material and share common frustrations before and after class if you're on friendly terms with other students. Every little bit of anxiety reduction helps.

• **Attending class regularly keeps philosophical issues at the forefront of your mind.** Not all learning is deliberate and conscious. Listening to your instructor's explanations and elaborations of textual material can trigger new connections for you, can spark your own creative ideas, and can identify areas of misunderstanding.

• **You benefit by others' questions and by following student-instructor interchanges.**

• **You're likely to improve your understanding of assigned readings after your instructor has discussed them with the class.** Don't rob yourself of this vital resource.

• When an instructor says that "attendance does not count," that only refers to his or her grading policy. Attendance always affects *your* learning.

• Whether or not you get specific credit toward a grade for attendance, most instructors are favorably impressed by regular, *attentive* attendance. Assigning grades is a complex process, and the difference between a B-minus and C-plus, for example, might be your instructor's unconscious sense of your class participation or attendance. (It is reasonable for instructors to conclude that students cannot have learned in-class course material covered in their absence, and thus not award the higher of two possible grades to those with significant absences.)

• Instructors need regular feedback from students. Most instructors modify their courses according to student response. Students' body language, comments, and questions are vital clues for gearing a course's content and pace to its audience. The reactions of students who just drop in now and then are not reliable indicators of a course's effectiveness.

> You will demand much of your teachers, but what you get is your responsibility.   *William H. Armstrong*

WHY SELF-RESPECT MATTERS

Everyone benefits from a pleasant classroom atmosphere. An essential component of a good learning environment is mutual respect. Instructors and students are equally entitled to courteous, respectful treatment from each other. Therefore, you have special responsibilities and obligations as a student. (Instructors also have special ethical obligations, but this is a student manual.) Further, I suggest that you *have a basic moral obligation to respect yourself.*

The following distinction between *self-respect* and *self-esteem* is not popular. It rests on subtle and complex notions regarding objectivity, self, character, and such. I can only present a sketch of it here; but I believe that even if you reject the distinction or are troubled by some of my suggestions, reflecting on the *possibility* that we have duties of self-respect is itself worthwhile.

Let me suggest, then, for your consideration, the possibility that *self-respect* differs from *self-esteem*. Many people seem unaware that *self-esteem only refers to our opinions of ourselves.* Self-esteem is entirely subjective. The harmful psychological effects of excessively low self-esteem are well known and highly publicized. You've probably studied "self-esteem issues" in other courses, perhaps even in grade school or high school. Unfortunately, much less attention has been paid to the harmful effects that result from lack of self-respect.

In clear contrast to self-esteem, *self-respect is the quality of valuing yourself for the right reasons.* In other words, self-respect begins with a commitment to truth, to *objectivity* and *integrity*. Self-respect cannot be reduced to subjective states because unhappy, confused, or emotionally unhealthy people can become acclimated to degrading conditions and behavior. Just as it is possible for a highly competent, talented individual to possess undesirably low self-esteem, so, too, it is possible for lazy, corrupt, or cruel individuals to think very highly of themselves.

Here's a simple analogy to help you understand what I mean. Persons addicted to smoking cigarettes get used to poisoning themselves. They "feel bad" when they take *objectively* good care of their bodies by not smoking. They "feel good" when they inhale toxins and sicken themselves—because their body chemistries are out of balance. In other words, subjective responses do not always reflect objective conditions. Just think of some decent, bright, wonderful person you know who "puts herself down," or fails to see her true abilities. Contrast such a person with some lazy, dishonest boor who just loves himself, who denies, distorts, or trivializes serious character defects. The boor may have an *inappropriately* high sense of self-esteem. Objectively, the modest self-deprecator—in spite of her feelings of self-doubt—behaves in ways that show self-respect.

Ideally, we want to respect and esteem ourselves honestly and wisely. Realistically, we can at least refuse to equate our subjective self-assessments with accurate pictures of who we are. Indeed, the so-called self-esteem movement, in its correct observation that many of us suffer from excessively low self-esteem, has reminded us that feelings alone are inadequate guides.

In blunt terms, then, the concept of self-esteem is unconnected to reality checking. Self-respect, on the other hand, is a function of personal integrity, and as such cannot be divorced from reality-testing or reduced to our feelings about ourselves. This is not to say that moral feelings do not play a role in manifesting self-respect, only that self-respect entails (1) accurate recognition of our capacities, commitments, rights, and duties, and (2) *behavior* that is generally and deliberately consistent with them.

> As important as our feelings about ourselves are, they do not completely reflect who we really are. We may feel badly about ourselves even though we work hard, meet our responsibilities, and take good care of ourselves—and we may feel just great about ourselves while behaving irresponsibly, or even cruelly, toward ourselves and others.

In one of the most influential works of modern moral philosophy, Immanuel Kant argued that respect for persons is one of the three basic principles that serve as the foundation of our specific moral obligations. In a famous passage, Kant frames what is known as the Principle of Dignity as an imperative: *"Act so that you treat humanity, whether in your own person or in that of another, always as an end and never as a means only."* (If you'd like to read more about Kant, see Chapter 10 of my introductory text *Archetypes of Wisdom*, Third Edition or any number of other excellent introductory philosophy or ethics texts.)

I am particularly impressed—and convinced—by Kant's insistence that we have a general, basic obligation not to treat ourselves as *means only*. To treat something as a means is to value it as a way to accomplish or acquire something else, that is, to value that thing *extrinsically*. When we treat something as *an end in and of itself*, we value it *intrinsically*—of and for itself. If you buy an antique vase because you believe it will increase in monetary value, your ultimate goal (end) is making money. The vase is a means to that end. You could just as easily have bought a spoon or quilt, if they could have more efficiently accomplished your goal. If, on the other hand, you buy an antique vase because you admire its beauty and have no intention of selling it later, then for you, the vase is an end-in-itself, not a means to something else. That specific vase has intrinsic value for you, value unique to that vase.

(And, of course, the vase may have both extrinsic and intrinsic value for you.)

Another, more significant way to grasp means-ends, extrinsic-intrinsic distinctions is to consider persons. If you are fortunate enough to love someone, that person has intrinsic value for you. I love my wife because she is exactly who she is—not as a means to financial security, not as a source of emotional support, or physical comfort. She may, indeed, be a means to many ends, but my love for her is not dependent on those ends. In other words, if she gets sick or loses her job, she does not "lose her value," the way a vehicle does when it malfunctions or an investment when it goes bad.

Now Kant understood that we all serve as means to various ends for one another. I am a means to credits in a philosophy course for my students, and they are means to a job and opportunities of expression to me. My plumber is a means to a repaired toilet for me, and I am a means to an enormous income to her. But Kant warned against reducing persons (ourselves as well as others) to mere means, to means only. His arguments are complex, and philosophers disagree over their soundness. Nonetheless, he makes a valuable observation, one echoed in other moral, religious, and philosophical work: Persons are not things. In Kantian language, you and I possess intrinsic worth (*dignity*) that entitles us to fundamental moral respect—and that *obligates us to show respect for ourselves and others.*

When we treat others with disrespect, we ignore or harm their dignity. We can do this in dramatic ways (murder, sexual assault, gross insults, and the like) or in more or less subtle ways (wasting other people's time, manipulating people, lying, cheating, and such). We can also disrespect ourselves through substance abuse, sexual promiscuity, wasting our own lives and time, reducing ourselves to workaholics, "fame-aholics," or "grade-aholics." Time wasted is life wasted, and none of us knows how much of that we have.

I suggest that by virtue of your college student status, you have a basic obligation—*to yourself and the community that provides your college opportunity*—to get as much value from your education as possible. On the most primitive level, you simply owe it to yourself not to waste your own time. On a more social level, no public college student, no student on financial aid, no student participating in any program funded by taxes, no student supported by his or her parents or others, *ever* pays for the *complete* cost of a college degree. This is especially true at state colleges and universities. Tuition does not cover the financial cost to the college of your education. Thus—directly or indirectly—your college education is supported by a larger community.

The ideal way to show respect and gratitude for the opportunity to get an education is to get yourself educated, to actively do everything in your power to benefit from your college time. In an ideal world, this would make you happier, healthier, and employable, which, in turn, would make your family, friends, and community happier and healthier. In the real world things are murkier. Nonetheless, *you* are almost certain to be much better off if you make the most out of college, and think in terms of owing yourself a great deal of solid self-respect.

Thinking in terms of *self-respect* instead of (or at least in addition to) *self-esteem*, will raise your sights and encourage you to do your honest best. Many of us know of individuals who are, so it appears, proud of "getting away" with things: buying term papers, cheating on tests, having friends sign roll sheets, never cracking (or owning) a textbook. It is psychologically possible for such persons to possess high self-esteem. Yet this kind of behavior sows disrespect and unease. Cheaters annoy honest students and cause some professors to abolish all attempts at stopping them or, at the opposite extreme, provoke totalitarian police-state type overreactions that result in hostile, chilly classroom dynamics. College classroom slackers treat themselves like unhappy junior-high school students, thereby adopting a standard beneath their actual (objective) status and abilities.

In the simplest terms: You are worthy of a good education. Because you are worthy of a good education, you owe it to yourself to do whatever it takes for you to be a good student. Being a good student does not require being a so-called perfect student. Some students with a 4.0 GPA (grade point average) cheat themselves out of a rich well-rounded education and sane social life. You must ultimately seek your own honest counsel here. In today's competitive world, you should strive to get the highest grades you can. But you must do so with an honest, realistic appraisal of your present life circumstances. What is realistic for a single student living with mom and dad and what is realistic for a single parent with two children and a full-time job are clearly not the same.

CAMPUS ETHICS

Your basic obligation to yourself includes giving each subject a real chance—because you are always developing and never know what new, unexpected path may reveal itself to you. Lack of effort and interest in this or that course may blind you to unrecognized abilities and interests that, once noted and nurtured, could add vigor and quality (even purpose) to your college years, as well as your later life.

From a fundamental obligation not to waste, trivialize, or "mediocritize" your life flow specific ethical habits that will enrich your educational experiences, and those of your fellow students and your professors.

> Unethical habits not only interfere with your education by fostering indolence, dishonesty, resentment, and alienation, they always cost more than they pay. The student who somehow manages to "get away" with cheating, skimming through Cliff's Notes®, buying term papers, last-minute cramming, and poor attendance, will have accomplished the tragic feat of graduating from college without an education.

The following guidelines rest on the premise that ethical behavior has both moral and practical benefits. In other words, it is to your personal advantage to behave ethically.

• **Be courteous in class.** Discourtesy pollutes the classroom, laboratory, or athletic field. Rude comments, hostile or disinterested body language, communicating with other students during lectures or while others have the floor, and so on, send a message (intentional or not) of indifference and contempt for others and for the educational activity in progress. Discourtesy distracts and disturbs serious students, students fulfilling their obligations to themselves and the learning community. Discourtesy may also draw the kind of attention to you that negatively affects your grades.

• **Don't cheat in any form.** Cheating is a form of theft. If cheating is widespread, it leads to general contempt for education, expertise, and certification. If many people get good grades they have not earned, the value of everyone's grade point average (and degree) is diminished. The more mediocre, marginally qualified, semi-literate college graduates there are, the less significance *your degree* will have because no one will know which category of graduates you fall into: informed, competent graduates, or mediocre, fraudulent ones.

• **Keep your commitments.** Your instructor has to budget his or her time, too. When you turn in late papers or ask to take tests late, you place extra demands on that time. Be sure you have very good reasons before doing that—and if you must have special consideration, be sure to fulfill whatever optional deadline or choice your instructor allows.

• **If you can't resist communicating with your friends during class, don't sit near them.** All discussion in class should relate to the class and be directed to the entire class (unless your instructor assigns you to small groups). Fidgeting, mumbling, or passing notes interferes with the concentration of others and deprives them of their very basic right to a congenial learning environment. It also prevents you from learning along with the rest of the class, which can increase or foster feelings of alienation, defensiveness, and boredom.

• **Arrive on time and remain for the entire period—unless you've made other arrangements with your instructor.** Wandering in and out of class on your own schedule cheapens the atmosphere of the course. As noted above, such conduct suggests indifference, if not contempt, for what's happening in class. Leaving in the middle of class is like walking away without explanation in the middle of a conversation—not a respectful or friendly thing to do. Making the effort to arrive on time is another way of reinforcing the message to yourself that your classes and degree are important to you, and that *you deserve a first-rate education and have the will to do what's necessary to get one.*

• **Don't show off.** Most of us are familiar with the student-as-star. This is the individual who has plenty to say at *every* class meeting. When one or two students dominate class time, the rest of the class grows resentful and may tune out whenever the student-as-star has the floor. You won't lose anything by giving less confident students a chance to partake in class discussions, too (and you will contribute to the class by your courtesy). It's best to avoid the extremes of excessive shyness and excessive demands for attention. (Don't stifle genuine interest, however. If you're truly bursting with comments and questions, make arrangements to meet with your instructor during office hours or other mutually convenient times.)

• **Don't ask foolish questions.** The old saying notwithstanding, there *are* foolish questions. Don't use class time to ask any question you can find the answer to by yourself. Don't ask questions if you have not been studying, because you won't have any idea whether or not the answers are in the reading. What are foolish questions? Asking how many tests there will be when that information is stated clearly on the course syllabus that you were given the first week of class. Asking the meaning of a term that's defined in the textbook. Asking what page X is on when that information is included in the index of your textbook. When you ask foolish questions, you steal time from others.

• **Don't ask "diminishing" questions.** A *"diminishing" question is any question asked to avoid doing your best.* Here are some examples of commonly asked diminishing questions: Do spelling and grammar count? Do I have to buy the textbook? Can I just write my papers, I don't like to type? The problem with diminishing questions is that they reinforce a concept of their asker as an overwhelmed student trying to do as little as possible.

If this seems like an unreasonably harsh position, consider some implications of the grammar and spelling question just used as an example. Granted, many of us are poor spellers, and it would seem that subject matter (content) should count most. Although, this is generally true, let's consider some implications of completely ignoring spelling and grammar. Do you honestly want to meet *lower standards* than were met by earlier generations of students (including, perhaps, your own instructor)? Indeed, at many colleges, it is still not too much to expect students in all subject areas to express themselves grammatically—and most students rise to the task. Why should you or your class be an exceptional group, unwilling to even attempt to meet the highest standards?

Why would you *want* to exempt yourself from the strenuous, but rewarding, effort necessary to be your very best?

Asking for special consideration due to genuine needs is not the same thing as asking diminishing questions. Of course what counts as a "genuine need" is not always clear. Here, we must rely on the integrity and insight of the parties involved. But that's true of most practical questions.

> Here's a rule of thumb to use for identifying *diminishing questions*: If the chief purpose of a question is to evade hard work, standards of achievement, or levels of responsibility that *the asker* has the *ability*—but not the *desire*—to meet, then the question diminishes the asker.

• **Don't sign up for classes unless you are reasonably sure you will complete them.** Many colleges today suffer from overcrowding. When a high-demand class is closed, students who need that class may find themselves forced to take less desirable alternatives or attend an extra term. If you drop out of such a class after the enrollment period is over, you've essentially wasted a valuable opportunity—and prevented anyone else from taking advantage of it. Dropping a class is not merely a personal matter.

• **Treat student evaluations of your professors with care.** Though you may not be aware of it, most instructors react to student evaluations. If a number of students praise a feature of the class, we are likely to continue it. If a number of students complain about the same thing, most instructors take it seriously. Student evaluations are your chance to help your instructor and his or her future students. If you have complaints, present them in a mature manner. Personal attacks and X-rated language tend to be dismissed as the immature reactions of failing students. Be specific. Tell us what is good or bad about the course and why.

CHAPTER 2

Reading Philosophy

*If you do not read good books you have no advantage over the
person who cannot read them.*

Mark Twain

M ost philosophical literature attempts to make a rational
case that will support a philosophical point of view. Even
when philosophical literature is emotionally powerful, creative,
and witty, aesthetic qualities take second place to the pre-
sentation of a philosophical argument.

As a rule, philosophers attempt to present tightly reasoned
chains of ideas leading from basic, initially clear, ideas to less obvious, more complex ones. One consequence of this noble goal is that
reading philosophical literature requires a high level of patience
and concentration. Because important points are connected to specific preceding points, you must not lose track of the line of reasoning. This takes effort and close concentration.

Philosophers often invent their own technical vocabulary in
an attempt to be both clear and fair. Sometimes philosophers coin
brand new words; other times they give their own special meanings to words already in use. *Failure to note the precise meaning of
key terms results in failure to follow the philosopher's line of reasoning.* Having to keep track of these technical philosophical
meanings can be difficult, but it cannot be avoided. Not all
philosophers are careful to define the unique meanings of key

terms. Philosophical readers must always be on the lookout for unusual uses of common terms as well as for newly coined terms.

Sometimes, philosophers even use the same term to mean different things—without warning the reader. *In addition to watching for the meaning of key terms, you must check to see that terms retain a consistent meaning.*

HEALTHY CONFUSION

Don't be surprised if your first reading of a philosophical text confuses you. I find that I must read most philosophical arguments at least twice, and often three times before I really *begin* to understand them.

When you find yourself confused and frustrated, remember that you are learning a new philosophical vocabulary as well as trying to identify a line of reasoning that may involve side-lines and sub-points. This requires a form of mental juggling. You must retain a number of isolated pieces of information until you can identify the overall structure of the argument.

Don't be surprised or intimidated if you initially feel confused by philosophy. Most of that confusion clears up if you merely persist, being as attentive as possible at each reading. You will often find that after a few pages of difficult reading, your comprehension suddenly improves. When that happens, it's a good idea to go back and immediately reread preceding relevant material.

QUICK TIPS FOR MORE EFFECTIVE READING

Here's a list of techniques and strategies that help many readers. Feel free to modify them according to your own reading experience. If, however, you find reading abstract or complex material difficult, or such material is new to you, it's probably a good idea to give these tips a try.

• **Always skim to get an overview.** Skim the table of contents of the book (or the headings in a chapter). Flip through articles, chapters, or sections using headings and subheadings to get a sense of organizational structure. Read the preface or introductory notes provided by the editor or author. Check to see if there is an index and glossary.

• **Begin with a general idea of the passage's main point and its strategy for establishing that point.** You can get this information from chapter summaries, from your instructor, and from other books and articles. (See the Beginning Philosopher's Bibliography at the end of this book.)

• **Read with a pencil, highlighter, or pad of self-sticking notes handy, and flag technical philosophical terms and important passages as you come across them.**

• **Read in good light.**

• **Find a comfortable spot away from distractions.** Some people study better with a little background music, others don't. Do what works for you. Pick a study spot that's good for your needs—and whenever possible always study in the same spot.

• **Make reading a priority.** If you become distracted by thoughts of other things you need to do, write them down to deal with after you are through reading. *Then*, tell yourself that this is your time to read. Stay focused on reading.

• **Suspend personal judgments and don't forget the principle of charity (see Chapter 1).** Completely ignore whether or not you like what is being claimed. Your initial readings should be only for comprehension. Evaluation should come later, because critical evaluation depends on clearly understanding what is being claimed and how that claim is being supported.

• **Use the glossary and a good unabridged dictionary.** Look up difficult words right away.

• **Consider buying a philosophical dictionary.** General reference dictionaries do not contain *technical* definitions of philosophical terms.

• **Read through an entire section in one sitting, even if you don't understand most of it.** After your first reading, you'll have a clearer idea of the structure of the argument or explanation. You'll be in good shape to reread more closely. You'll understand much more on the second reading because you know how points made in one part of the passage relate to points made elsewhere. You'll also know what's most important, and why.

• **Take regular breaks that are long enough to clear your mind and give your eyes a rest.** Stop reading often enough to prevent fatigue. Don't consciously think about what you've just read. Move around, stretch. Let your unconscious mind process the material.

• **Reread as often as** *you* **need to.** Don't fall into the trap of comparing your study needs to others.

• **Vary your reading speed.** As a general rule, you need to read important, technically difficult passages at a slower rate than less complex informational passages.

• **Pause regularly to see if you can clearly restate difficult passages in your own words.** Don't just assume that you understand something because you're not having any noticeable trouble reading it. Forcing yourself to restate important ideas at regular intervals is an effective way of testing comprehension.

• **Reread difficult passages in a different way.** You may find that you have to take one sentence at a time when reading especially complex or poorly written technical passages. You may need to look up the meanings of two or three words in one paragraph. *Whatever you do, don't merely repeat the kind of reading that's not working.*

• **When you're in a rut, flag and skip unusually difficult passages; return to them later.** Don't spend so much time and effort on one difficult passage that you get completely confused, frustrated, and dispirited. If careful rereading isn't working, continue with the rest of the chapter. This often clarifies the difficult passage.

• **Ask your instructor to recommend some supplementary reading for especially difficult passages.** If the preceding tip doesn't work, consult another text that deals with the same point. Sometimes just reading a different explanation will clear things right up. There are many excellent philosophy textbooks and reference books available.

• **Don't confuse a tired mind or body with reading difficulties.** If everything you're reading suddenly makes no sense, or you encounter an especially difficult passage at the end of a long day or study session, you may just be too tired to benefit from more work. Get some rest.

• **Perform routine maintenance.** Don't get too hungry, thirsty, or tired. Avoid all alcohol, and avoid all illegal drugs because drugs and alcohol inhibit comprehension skills.

• **After you've given all these tips a fair try, ask your instructor for additional help.** Sometimes one more clarification or explanation is all it takes to unlock the meaning of a difficult passage.

• **Make sure you don't have a reading or comprehension problem.** If you are having reading difficulties in most of your classes, consult a counselor. There are simple, free tests your school can provide that can identify common, *manageable* reading and comprehension difficulties.

• **If your counselor or instructor recommends the college reading lab, take advantage of its tutorial services.** Don't be too embarrassed to get help if you need it. The folks at the reading lab want to help you succeed on your own. They will not embarrass you or make you dependent on them. Think of them like P.E. coaches: You will do all the work and earn all the credit; they will help you develop better skills.

BEYOND THE TEXTBOOK

Although your textbook is probably your primary source of detailed subject matter information, it does not have to be your only source. Develop the habit of taking full advantage of all appropriate resources. Become a study artisan, using a full set of special tools.

• **Use this book!** Hang on to *How to Get the Most Out of Philosophy* and review it when you need a study pep talk or a little friendly encouragement.

• **Maximize your use of your philosophy textbook.** Use all of its pedagogical (teaching and learning) features: chapter introductions, summaries, study questions, glossaries, index, chapter headings, and so forth.

• **Take advantage of any study guides, student manuals, CD-ROMS or computerized aids available for your textbook, or prepared and distributed by your instructor.** Don't be too "hip" or "cool" to use these features. Among their advantages, four stand out: (1) They *focus your attention* on key ideas, figures, and so forth. (2) They require *active reading*. (3) They involve *repetition*. (4) The best study guides involve *written responses*.

• **Regularly check your comprehension by writing down your own summary of a section's key points and arguments in your own words.** Check your summary against the text. If you can accurately and thoroughly summarize a position, you understand it. *If you cannot accurately and thoroughly summarize a position, you do not understand it*. Period. This is the best self-test you can perform for comprehension. It's important because, as you know, you cannot analyze or evaluate an idea until you can understand it without distorting it.

• **Ask your friends to grade your summaries (see preceding tip), and offer to grade theirs.** This exercise is another opportunity for *active reading and thinking*. It develops concentration and comprehension.

• **Discuss the reading material with others.** One of the best ways of testing comprehension is by refining your understanding of an idea or argument by verbally expressing it in your own words to someone else.

• **Use the library.** Most college libraries have copies of the *Encyclopedia of Philosophy*, and a variety of philosophical history books and commentaries, as well as other philosophy textbooks. Ask your instructor to recommend supplemental reading. It's also a good idea to just browse through the philosophy stacks (section of shelves). If you try reading two or three different authors' treatments of the same issues, you'll probably find they're each especially helpful in different ways.

• **Consult reference and technical sources.** See the Beginning Philosopher's Bibliography at the back of this book, and consult the bibliography of your textbook for the names of good reference books. Talk to your college library's reference librarian.

PART TWO

Critical Thinking, Reading, And Writing

When the destroyer comes, his first act is to burn the books.

Thomas More

Perhaps the most valuable product of a good education is the development of a critical attitude. In this context, "critical" does not mean negative or hostile. From the Greek root *kritikes*, meaning "to judge" or "to discern," a critical attitude is one that does not take things at face value, and that demands reasonable proof before accepting or rejecting claims.

Developing a healthy critical attitude is an important function of any philosophy course. Initially, your professor's demand for critical responses can be frustrating, especially if you have not had much practice carefully analyzing and justifying your opinions by making a rational case for them. But critical thinking, reading, and writing are vital student skills that can be developed and polished like many other skills.

Chapter 3 is a basic overview of critical thinking. Chapters 4 and 5 apply critical thinking skills and principles to reading and writing.

CHAPTER 3

Developing A
Critical Attitude

The student who ignores rules and definitions is all too soon over-
come by ideas that cannot be understood.

William H. Armstrong

The term "critical thinking" is widely used in educational circles. You're probably already familiar with it. Here is a list of some of the chief characteristics of critical thinking:

• **Critical thinking is the conscious, deliberate rational assessment of claims according to clearly identified standards of proof.** Although appropriate standards of proof vary, depending on the nature of the claim, certain fundamental principles of reasoning apply to all critical thinking. These include standards of relevance, consistency, reasonableness (likeliness to be true), and sufficiency. Any claim that rests on inconsistent evidence, inconsistencies between premises and their conclusions, circularity, or ambiguity must be recast or rejected.

• **Critical thinking is objective and impersonal, while recognizing that personal experience and emotion play a part in the**

39

thoughtful assessment of claims. Critical thinking is *impersonal* in the sense that mathematics is impersonal. The truth of the sentence "2 + 2 = 4" is not a function of some particular person's moods, values, religion, gender, race, or such. The logical correctness of this pattern of reasoning is similarly *impersonal*:

> If   A   is greater than B, and
> If   B   is greater than C, and
> If   C   is greater than D, *then*
>   A   is greater than D.

• **Critical thinking offers sustained argumentation (verifiable, rational evidence) for claims supported by logical reasoning, expert testimony, language analysis, and appropriate personal and professional experience.** Good critical thinking presents a chain of reasons that will allow any interested, rational person to follow the evidence step by step to a rationally sustainable conclusion. Critical thinkers provide "whys" as well as "whats." That is, they explain why a position is worth holding or should be rejected in a fashion that allows others to follow their *reasoning process*. Basic critical thinking skills are the foundation of more specialized forms of logical analysis, scientific, or technical thinking. Basic critical thinking skills are useful in all walks of life, and are one of our best defenses against "self-imposed tutelage," blind prejudice, and avoidably foolish life choices.

> Critical thinking alerts us to what is sometimes referred to as the *public dimension of argument*. This means that the process used to arrive at conclusions is not mysterious or secret; it is subject to *public scrutiny* or *public verification* in much the same way that scientific experiments are presented in a way that enables other scientists to verify them. Thus, rational discourse is public discourse, and critical thinking has social and civic aspects, as well as logical and rational ones.

• **Critical thinking involves** *rational discourse,* **the use of reason to order, clarify, identify, and articulate our basic views of reality and truth according to agreed upon standards of evidence.** The ancient Greek philosopher **Socrates (c. 470-399 BC)** gave his name to one famous form of rational discourse known as the **Socratic**

method. Many philosophy professors, and most law schools, use the Socratic method of teaching to foster critical thinking abilities in their students. *The Socratic method is a question-and-answer technique in which the teacher uses guided, sometimes pointed, questions that require the pupil to reason out appropriate answers.* The Socratic method demands more than just the retention and regurgitation of information—it requires the critical analysis of opinions by carefully defining key terms, drawing inferences, identifying key principles, patterns, and connections, and so forth. Socrates thought that it was very important that the pursuit of truth be public and social so that each participant could function as a monitor for other participants. In that way, our individual blind spots could be recognized and filled in by others. In my opinion, one of the most optimistic and charming aspects of Socrates was his insistence that no matter what conclusion was reached by this process (and often the conclusion was that so far nobody is completely correct), everyone benefits—especially those whose errors are identified. Socrates thought that the wise (rational) person will be grateful to anyone who improves his or her thinking. In other words, Socrates was more interested in getting closer to the truth than he was in his image or "ego." From his perspective, rational discourse is a social good, and all true patriots participate in it, because a healthy democracy depends on enlightened citizens. If that's true, then good critical thinking skills are to everyone's advantage.

- **Critical thinking is coherent, following the evidence where it leads, in an orderly manner.** One of the signs of good critical thinking is the willingness to accept the best evidence, even when it requires modifying or rejecting a cherished belief or highly desired conclusion. To cite just one famous example of the significance of good critical skills to the quality of civic life, consider the widely followed O. J. Simpson criminal trial of 1995. During the countless discussions of this famous case, many legal experts publicly expressed concern over what one of them characterized as a "growing, serious lack of rationality" among jurors in all parts of the country. Both prosecutors and defense lawyers expressed concern over whether or not jurors willfully disregarded evidence and legally binding instructions, choosing to vote with their feelings or instincts. The issue here is not just whether this particular jury's vote was "correct," but the fact that so many commentators were concerned that more and more jurors increasingly exhibit blatant indifference to providing and responding to clearly articulated reasons, thereby interfering with the process of *deliberation*. *Deliberation requires the rational assessment of evidence through forthright discussion and civil argumentation.*

In other words, a growing number of practicing lawyers and judges are reporting their fears that many of our fellow citizens either cannot or will not engage in the give-and-take of rational discourse. Such individuals are uncritical thinkers, willing to make serious choices without taking the time, or exerting the effort, to evaluate all sides of an issue critically. (Do you see similar indifference, even hostility, to civil rational discourse among politicians? in some of your classes? in your personal life?)

WHAT IS *UNCRITICAL* THINKING?

• **Uncritical thinking is characterized by lack of precision and lack of coherence.** Student essays sometimes suffer from poor critical thinking skills when they rely on vague claims to sustain their arguments. Basic ways to be precise include using correct technical terms and examples found in your reading, and writing clearly focused sentences. You should also avoid using pontificating or pretentious language. If you are not comfortable reading a sentence out loud, it may be because it's unclear.

• **Uncritical thinking substitutes strong feelings for clearly stated evidence.** Whether you're a television fan or not, you've probably seen enough talk shows to recognize how commonly volume and aggressiveness substitute for rational discourse. Guests and invited "experts" shout each other down, all talk at once, sneer, point, gesture wildly—none of which have any bearing on having a good point. Even if these methods "work" in the sense of persuading lots of people, they do not get us closer to the truth. If that were not bad enough, these common substitutes for civilized rational discourse probably breed cynicism and hostility. Advertisers and campaigning politicians can also assault us with uncritical, emotionally powerful substitutes for good reasons.

• **Uncritical thinking is often defensive, reacting to criticism in inappropriate ways.** It can be very difficult to accept criticism. Even if your critic makes good points, you might be tempted to defend your "ego," to "save face," by going on the attack. One common strategy here is to zero in on the critic's faults, or identify ulterior motives or ill will behind the criticism. Your position cannot, however, be strengthened by pointing out flaws in someone else, questioning their motives, and so forth. Watch out for this one.

• **Uncritical thinking confuses winning debates and popularity with being right.** Because we are such a results-oriented society, it's tempting to reduce all considerations to "Does it work?" Thus, we're tempted to admire the sleazy trick that sways the jury—and overlook the fact that our legal system suffers as we become convinced that it's all just an elaborate "game." Your philosophy professor is not going to be like most people. He or she has devoted years to the study of careful reasoning, logic, critical thinking, methods of persuasion, and so forth. What looked pretty clever in a Presidential Debate, or on the Oprah Winfrey or Crossfire television shows, may not work at all in your philosophy class.

• **Uncritical thinking is often impulsive, based on instantaneous judgments strongly influenced by personality, race, gender, religion, political affiliation, or deeply felt psychological needs.** We've all seen other people do this. Sometimes, you can almost see a kind of screen fall over their faces, indicating that nothing anyone says or does will get them to reconsider their position. When people are in this state, they are not rational. That is, reasons have no effect on their point of view.

• **Uncritical thinking confuses** *willed ignorance* **with knowledgeable confidence.** *Willed ignorance is an attitude of indifference to the possibility of error or enlightenment.* Willed ignorance holds onto beliefs regardless of the facts. You can recognize willed ignorance by such expressions as: "I don't care what anybody says, I know X." "Nothing anybody says will ever change my mind about X." "You might be right, but I don't care. I'm going to believe X." People in the throes of willed ignorance refuse to read the literature of their opponents: "No, I've never taken any courses in evolution, I don't have to. I just know those scientists are wrong." "I've never listened to Rush Limbaugh, because he's a bigot." In a nutshell, willed ignorance is unresponsive to reasons, facts, and evidence that challenge preferred points of view.

> Simply put, uncritical thinking accepts or rejects claims according to momentary impulses, unquestioned loyalties, and unreflective personal bias.

WHAT DOES CRITICAL THINKING REQUIRE?

• **Critical thinking requires the application of appropriate standards of evidence.** What counts as adequate evidence in an informal conversation will probably not be adequate for a philosophy class discussion. Similarly, what's adequate for a class discussion will not be adequate for an essay or term paper.

• **Critical thinking requires intellectual maturity.** Good critical thinkers do not allow their feelings and personal preferences to control their judgment. When criticized, the critical thinker always asks: Is this criticism valid? If it is, she modifies her original position, since her goal is truth, not mere face saving.

• **Critical thinking takes *work*.** Important issues require careful study. You cannot make reasonable *decisions* if you do not study issues for yourself—all you can do is react based on partial, secondhand opinions and untested beliefs and prejudices.

• **Critical thinking requires practice.** Athletes and artists have to work regularly to maintain a certain level of proficiency. Critical thinking skills also require regular "thinking workouts."

• **Critical thinking requires courage.** It can be difficult to ask "How do you know that?" People sometimes resent being asked to prove their claims. They may be insulted because we don't merely accept what they say because they're our friends or relatives.

They may be defensive because our questions reveal that they don't have good reasons for their assertions. Sometimes people don't have *any reasons* for their assertions.

• **Critical thinking requires tact.** Because we depend on one another in our search for truth, it's always best to avoid asking questions in a way that's likely to turn discussions into personal disputes. Angry exchanges reduce, rather than enlarge, our fund of information. The most effective critical thinkers do not shy away from asking necessary questions or pointing out important errors, but they do so with respect and courtesy, fully aware that they might be wrong themselves. As a very general rule, people tend to respond better to clearheaded, focused assertiveness than to self-righteous aggression or unshakable willed ignorance.

CRITICAL THINKING PRACTICES THAT PAY OFF IN THE CLASSROOM—AND BEYOND

• **Distinguish what is important from what is not according to regularly re-evaluated principles.** Just as it is unwise to treat important issues as matters of mere preference, it is unwise to subject all issues to a single, excessively detailed analysis. *Hairsplitting* is the name some philosophers give to the error of uncritically excessive analysis of minor points, as if they were major ones. By distinguishing what is important from what is not, good critical thinkers don't get bogged down in a quagmire of tedious minutiae.

• **Pay careful attention to the meanings of terms.** Philosophy is a language-intensive subject. Complex ideas and complex arguments are basic to most philosophical (and all sophisticated) writing. Philosophy, like most academic subjects, has its own technical vocabulary. Many of these technical terms are based on non-English roots. Here are some examples of technical philosophical language: dialectic, noumena, phenomena, eudaimonia, entelechy, a priori, a posteriori, mystification, contradiction, ontological, valid, circular, tautology. You are not unintelligent if you do not know what they mean. You are *ignorant* in the sense of simply lacking experience and knowledge of these terms. You certainly wouldn't try to take a French test without learning some French. If you don't speak French, there is one sense in which you "don't know" what it means to say, *"La plume de ma tante est sur la table."* Once you make the translation to "My aunt's pen is on the table," everything clears up. The *concept* is readily understood once the *language* is understood.

• **Be sure you understand exactly what is being said before you do anything else.** One of the most common mistakes students make is trying to evaluate a claim without first understanding exactly what is being said. For instance, a student once came by my office and said, "I'm having trouble understanding what Aristotle means by *eudaimonia.*" "All right," I said, "why don't you just tell me what the word *eudaimonia* means." "That's the problem!" he exclaimed. "I can't understand what Aristotle means." "How could you," I asked, "if you have no idea whatsoever what the word itself means?" I sent the student away with specific pages to read in our textbook, pages that had been assigned over a week earlier, and which included a definition and explanation of *eudaimonia*—which, incidentally, is a term Aristotle used to refer to fully realized existence, a state of being fully aware, vital, and alert. It is often translated as "happiness," but happiness is probably too restrictive for the fullness Aristotle had in mind. If my student had said, "I'm not sure what it means to be 'fully realized'," I could have helped him. But he had not done his homework, literally and figuratively. The bottom line is that critical thinking is always about something: terms, facts, causal claims, and so forth. There is no short cut through memorizing and understanding. Oh yes, after reading the material with attentiveness and care, my student had no trouble understanding *eudaimonia* well enough to write a clear essay commenting on Aristotle's conception of happiness. Don't confuse being poorly prepared with an inability to understand.

Although it can be frustrating to "just memorize" definitions and details, it's actually a good idea to force yourself to memorize the meanings of new terms—whether you completely understand them or not. Failure to attend to this basic task can create confusion about being confused! I've lost count of the times students have told me that they do not understand what a concept means only to discover that they have failed to familiarize themselves with the essential vocabulary of the day's lesson.

- **Rely on relevant expertise when appropriate.** No one can possess significant knowledge of all of the kinds of issues that confront people. Socrates insisted that the search for truth cannot begin until we honestly acknowledge the limits of our own knowledge. You can maximize your critical thinking efforts by taking advantage of the accumulated knowledge of experts. *Just be sure that any experts you consult possess expertise in the field in question, and that most other qualified experts agree with them.* Even if you do not know the particulars of a given subject area, you can still apply careful thought to selecting the experts you rely on.

- **Question any claim that is fundamentally inconsistent with your own carefully evaluated experience (including claims from experts).** I keep a file of deceptive and bogus advertisements. One of my favorites is a flyer for a book of "exam secrets" that *guarantees* a "great GPA" with no effort. I don't know about your experience, but I've never seen anything capable of *guaranteeing* a great grade point average (GPA). Don't you think that such a "secret" would sweep the nation—no, sweep the world? The same goes for hair restorers, pills that melt away ugly fat while you sleep (Don't take too many!), 200-mile-per-gallon gadgets to add to your car, and $50.00 Rolex watches for sale in the cafeteria.

- **Analyze the motives of all interested parties (including your own), without reducing critical scrutiny to character analysis.** Contrary to common opinion, a person's intentions or motives do not tell us much about the reliability of their claims and arguments. When you uncover hidden biases or ulterior motives, you have an additional reason to scrutinize a claimant's assertions. But it is the asserted evidence that needs to be evaluated, not the arguer.

- **Distinguish between the arguer and the argument.** A variety of logical fallacies stem from confusing arguers with their arguments. Perhaps the best known is the **argumentum ad hominem,** literally "argument against the man," but now more commonly known as the **personal attack.** The most blatant form of personal attack is the **character assassination:** "You should reject the President's balanced budget proposal because he has been unfaithful to his wife." A more subtle—and so more dangerous—version of the personal attack is the **circumstantial personal attack:** "We can ignore Professor Wadsworth's argument supporting a woman's right to abortion on demand. The professor's husband owns an abortion clinic." The *tu quoque* or **"look who's talking"** is another common form of confusing the arguer with the argument: "You're a fine one to tell me to quit smoking. You could stand to lose a few pounds." Notice that in each of these examples, the character and motives of the arguers do not—of themselves—have any bearing on whether or not the positions being advocated are sound. The President may have unacceptable personal behavior *and at the same time* advocate a wise budget. Professor Wadsworth's argument may be solid, even if the *motive* for making it is blind loyalty to her husband. Whether or not my friend is overweight, I should rationally consider his argument against smoking.

- **Respect differing points of view when they are reasonably defended.** A big problem with contempt for views with which we disagree is that we close ourselves off from the opportunity to learn and grow. (I would certainly hate to think that I will not change any of my fundamental beliefs one tiny bit for the rest of my life.)

- **Encourage rational discourse by allowing those with whom you disagree to present their point of view for themselves.** This means not interrupting those whose views we abhor by shouting them down before they've finished making their point. Being "correct" is not always enough, if in the process of expressing our views we generate hostility to rational discourse or substitute verbal abuse or physical force for intelligent defense of our views. Everybody loses when issues are decided by coercion or the loudest voice.

- **Welcome legitimate criticism by remaining open to the possibility of error.** If truth is what you seek, then you need to know the weaknesses in your ideas in order to improve them or set them aside as unsalvageable. "Playing ostrich" by attempting to avoid criticism does nothing to strengthen a position. A person with cancer has cancer whether or not a doctor diagnoses cancer. Remaining in "denial" may prevent curing a curable condition. Refusing to consider clear, fair criticism does nothing to strengthen your own case, and may harm your sense of self-respect. A confident truth-seeker has no reason to fear criticism. A lazy or fearful thinker will, however, be afraid of anything that will require effort or serious reassessment of a cherished belief.

- **Ask important and relevant questions tactfully and at appropriate times—and wait for a complete answer.** Asking questions serves a twofold purpose: (1) The question and answer process can refine and clarify a position. (2) Asking questions and listening to answers keeps the questioner alert and mentally active.

- **Suspend judgment until** *both sides* **of an issue have been given a fair hearing.** This requires being genuinely open to all reasonable, relevant evidence, and commits us to more than just token listening designed to create an impression of fairness. If I've already decided before you present your case, then even though I appear to be listening, I'm not really *hearing* you. Here's one more reminder to practice the principle of charity; it opens us up to a wider range of resources and improves our chances of making wise decisions.

- **Devote enough time to** *research* **vital issues for yourself.** Avoid relying on the mass media or authority figures for information or viewpoints. For the most part, the mass media are not reliable sources of important factual or technical information. If you want information about health care, vitamins, abortion ethics, race relations, educational patterns, and so forth, you will need to consult textbooks, professional journals, and various experts. Sales brochures put out by health food companies make claims that need to be verified against independent sources. Statistics cited by "prolife" and "pro-choice" advocates need to be checked—and so on and on. To repeat, critical thinking is an *activity*, it takes *work*.

• **Regularly remind yourself that those you disagree with believe that they are being reasonable.** Socrates thought that all evil results from ignorance. He argued that no one willingly chooses evil. I'm not sure he's completely correct, but I do think that most people want to be reasonable, that is, want to have good reasons. At any rate, *it's probably best for us to act as if others want to be rational.* This humanizes our ideological opponents and reminds us that most of us are fellow travelers in the search for wisdom, truth, and happiness. More often than not, respect for others reduces stress in our own lives. Note, however, that respect for others as serious truth seekers is not the same thing as naive or gullible acceptance of every idea as plausible. Nor is respecting others an excuse not to keep looking for more truth ourselves.

• **Make a sustained effort to get information from a variety of reliable sources.** I am reminded of a fascinating student I once had in a philosophy class, a very intelligent man in his mid-fifties. He was absolutely convinced that the Holocaust of World War II was a big hoax. Nothing I, nor any of his other professors, said or showed him changed his mind. He fell back on his very considerable and expensive library of history books, all supporting his odd contention. This man worked hard to sustain his belief. He read literally hundreds of books—very carefully. When I pointed out that most of these books were published by six companies, three of which had the same address, he just shrugged. The moral of the story is that no quantity of biased or weak evidence somehow becomes good evidence. One way of sustaining a position of willed ignorance is to exert precious effort in a blind cause.

THREE BASIC STANDARDS OF EVIDENCE

• *Relevance*: Evidence offered to support a claim must be directly related to establishing the truth of that claim.

> **Two examples of irrelevant evidence:**
> (1) Buying a product because it is a best seller. The fact that millions of people buy X has no direct bearing on whether or not *you* should buy X.

(2) Rejecting or accepting a claim because you don't like the person making it. The sanitary habits, moral character, religious beliefs, race, age, gender, and social status of a person are not reasons for you to reject or accept his or her claims.

• *Reasonableness*: **Evidence offered to support a claim must be of such a nature that a disinterested rational person with relevant knowledge and expertise would accept it.**

Two examples of unreasonable claims:
(1) Claiming that the earth is flat. In order to sustain such a belief, you must somehow discount the consensus among qualified scientific experts that the earth is not flat. This can only be done by assuming that the vast majority of these experts are wrong, or that they are involved in a conspiracy. Both assumptions are unreasonable.

(2) Claiming that the "medical establishment" can cure cancer but won't because doctors, hospitals, and drug companies make so much money treating it. This claim is an example of the kind of conspiracy theory that flies in the face of experience. It requires that we believe that doctors and scientists would hide the discovery of a cure for cancer rather than publish it and win worldwide acclaim, an almost guaranteed Nobel prize, tons of money for research grants, and a place in medical history. Further, such theories require the unreasonable assumption that thousands of people can or will keep such an important secret for years. Lastly, the claim reduces all members of the medical establishment to greedy, money-hungry opportunists.

• *Sufficiency*: **There must be enough reasonable, relevant evidence to support the claim.**

Two examples of insufficient evidence:
(1) Drawing conclusions about members of other ethnic groups based only on your own experiences with them, and what you learn from the mass media. Even the most sociable and sophisticated among us do not have enough personal experience to draw conclusions about entire ethnic groups. The mass media present images carefully selected and edited for dramatic or novelty appeal. The mass media cannot be relied on to provide a thorough, representative view of life.

(2) Deciding that philosophy is boring based on your experiences with one course. One course from one instructor is simply not sufficient to draw conclusions about a subject.

One example of a claim that is both unreasonable and insufficient: The student described above who denied the existence of the Holocaust based on his extensive reading of hundreds of volumes of biased literature. By only consulting books from a few publishers with an ax to grind, this man, in effect, limited the scope of his support. A million dollars in play money is not sufficient to buy one dollar's worth of apples.

CHAPTER 4

Critical Reading

Reading is to the mind what exercise is to the body.

Joseph Addison

E ffective readers apply critical thinking skills to what they read, taking advantage of a variety of clues and strategies that simplify the process of understanding and evaluating different kinds of writing.

Critical reading skills can be learned and refined by most motivated readers. Philosophical writing, like most technical literature, poses special problems that can be greatly reduced by the application of a few basic principles of effective critical reading.

If you can remember lots of information about things that you're personally interested in, you have the basic ability to remember facts about philosophers, new technical terms, the titles of important books—and the due dates for all your assignments and tests. Even if philosophy is more difficult to read, *spending as much time* reading philosophy as reading about sports or movies or fashions will eventually make reading philosophy easier. Motivation and effort are important parts of ability. Critical reading skills can be developed by regular, focused work.

USE YOUR TEXTBOOKS' ORGANIZATIONAL FEATURES

• **Always read the preface.** Reading the preface is like having a little chat with the author of your textbook. The preface usually includes a brief description of the book's special features and why the author thinks they will help readers. Reading the preface will familiarize you with the author's "voice," the special style he or she has. Lastly, the preface may identify the author's chief goals and philosophical principles.

• **Get to know your textbook right away.** Read the table of contents. Quickly read one or two brief passages that catch your interest. Note margin quotations, boxed passages, illustrations, summaries of main points, study questions, index, and another special features designed to make the book more accessible, interesting, or understandable.

• **Take full advantage of margin quotes, boxed or off-set passages.** Such features will have been carefully selected because they are especially interesting, well-written, or unusual. Don't skip by them, enjoy them.

• **Familiarize yourself with the glossary (a list of definitions of key terms).** The glossary can be at the end of the text, at the beginning or end of chapters or sections, in the margins, or in some combination.

• **Study section headings.** Notice how they organize the text and provide clues about content. Text headings are like levels in an outline. In addition to labeling text sections, they classify and categorize them.

• **Before you read a chapter, review the table of contents.** If your textbook has a full table of contents, it will show the various levels of headings and subheadings in each chapter. Looking at such a table of contents is like looking at an outline. Knowing the structure of a chapter will aid in understanding its content.

• **Use section headings to organize your notes.** Some students find it helpful to list the chapter headings on sheets of note paper, allowing lots of room between headings. This provides a structure for lecture or reading notes. Of course you can always modify notes by adding organizational categories. The point is—to repeat—that you find some way of remaining an *active reader and notetaker.*

• **Use special features such as chapter summaries and study question to focus your reading.** Read summaries and study questions *early* in your study of a chapter. They flag important concepts that you need to understand—and that are likely to turn up on tests.

• **Take your text to class regularly so that you can follow along with the instructor if he or she refers to it.**

• **Use self-sticking notes to flag *every* passage you find difficult.** If a passage remains unclear after careful rereading, ask your instructor to go over it with you.

THE VIRTUES OF OWNING AND ANNOTATING YOUR OWN TEXT

Annotations are notes and comments written in the margins of a text by a reader. Though some people find it difficult to write in their books, annotating a text is a valuable study aid. Besides allowing you to annotate as you read, owning your own book allows you to study when it is most convenient. Of course you shouldn't annotate a text that you don't own.

• **Annotating a text prohibits passive reading, and draws you into a meaningful conversation with other minds.** Annotating is a lot like a conversation conducted in writing. If you have ever looked through a book that's been annotated, you know how personal and interesting annotations can be. Looking through a book that has been annotated by someone else can be like observing another person's thinking process. The very activity of annotating a text requires you to respond to what you're reading: to inquire, praise, criticize, express delight or astonishment. As you review your own annotated text, you will probably refine your critique by reacting to your own annotations. Every time you review, rehash, react, and respond, you are polishing and improving your understanding of what you read. Annotating a text makes it yours in a special way. You create your own handy reference notes to use in class, reviewing for tests, or researching essays or term papers.

• **Be critical, in a simple way.** Note "Yes," or "No," or even "B.S.," or "Wow!"—anything that works to get you involved in a dialogue with the text can help you better understand what you're reading.

• **If at all possible, buy your text with money you have *earned* or have borrowed (and will *repay* with money *you earn*).** Spending your own money on the text is a way to reinforce your commitment to success in the class.

• **What if you can't afford to purchase a text?** Most colleges have financial aid and short-term emergency loans available for students who cannot afford to buy necessary supplies. Taking the time and effort to secure aid or a loan is another way of reinforcing your commitment to success in a class.

> *Won't annotating a text diminish its resale value?* **It probably will. But you have to decide how important succeeding in a particular class (and in college in general) is to you. If your only choice is between reselling your books and eating or dropping out of college, then perhaps you should not write in your books. But if you somehow can afford to rent videos, go to concerts, buy cokes and beer, order a pizza, buy CD's, and so forth, then you can afford to annotate your text—by giving up some of these luxuries for a time.**

OUR BASIC READING STRATEGY SUMMARIZED

• Skim the table of contents of each chapter to get an overview of what's in it.

• Read chapter summaries and review questions next. (You might want to make a copy of the review questions to use as you study the chapter.)

• Browse through the assigned sections, reading whatever catches your eye, including margin quotes and boxed passages.

• Read the assignment once without worrying about taking notes or studying it carefully. Remember to keep reading even if you think that you don't understand anything. You'll be surprised later to discover that you've picked up more than you realized.

• Early in this process, make note of all new terms, and learn their definitions.

• Read the assignment a second time, more carefully. Keep your self-sticking notes and a copy of the review questions handy. Write out answers to study questions. Flag difficult passages.

• Write the page numbers of passages that pertain to review questions next to the questions themselves.

• Begin making your own marginal notations at this stage. Ask questions, jot down key ideas or terms that you'll want easy access to again. Make critical observations.

• If necessary, reread the text a third time.

• **Test your comprehension of key passages by restating them in your own words.** The best way to do this is by discussing the subject with another class member, friend, or relative. If that's not possible, pretend you are writing a letter to a friend in which you want to explain a particular passage. If you cannot restate a passage in your own words, you don't understand it.

WHAT TO DO IF NOTHING'S WORKING SO FAR

If you find it impossible to understand assigned readings after carefully following the steps discussed so far, you should consult your instructor and, probably, a counselor. You may discover that you need special classes in reading before you can succeed in philosophy. Take advantage of reading tests, reading labs, and related programs, if you need them.

Weak reading skills will not mysteriously disappear. Besides feeling frustrated and depressed because you cannot do as well as you want to, weak reading skills often result in low grades and serious long-term consequences.

Don't ignore a reading problem. Confront it as soon as you suspect its presence. Many times, special classes can quickly boost your performance. A wide variety of special programs are available for students with reading and learning difficulties.

CHAPTER 5

Critical Writing

Once, when Ernest Hemingway's son Patrick asked his father to edit a story Patrick had written, Hemingway carefully went through the manuscript, and returned it to his son. "But, Papa," Patrick complained, "you've only changed one word."

"If it's the right word, that's a lot," said Hemingway.

The primary goals of critical writing are *argumentation, analysis* and *evaluation*. Critical writing justifies a conclusion or interpretation by providing reasonable, relevant, and sufficient evidence to support it. The nature of the evidence depends on the specific way you choose to make your case, and can include any combination of documented appeals to authoritative sources, language analysis, comparison and contrast, logical argumentation, and appeals to experience.

Creative writing, by contrast, values novelty, personal expression, imagination, and emotional impact, among other things. *Expository writing* focuses on presenting information in an organized, useful manner. Creative, expository, and critical writing often occur in the same text.

BASIC FEATURES OF GOOD CRITICAL WRITING

Most philosophy courses involve critical writing assignments of varying complexity and scope. They might include brief essay-type test questions, out-of-class essays, and longer term paper assignments. Certain common features apply to all good critical writing, regardless of length.

• **Good critical writing clearly identifies its main point (thesis) early.** Your reader should not have to read three or four pages or paragraphs to figure out what your main point is (or worse yet, have to *guess*). Your thesis (main point) should be clear in the opening paragraph.

• **Good critical writing avoids evasive weasel claims.** The primary function of a weasel claim is to leave its author a way around criticism. Weasel claims make and evade a point at the same time. Consider this example: "It seems to me that Plato might have meant Z." Take a stand. Think. Did Plato mean Z or not?

• **Good critical writing documents its case so that readers can verify all important factual and scholarly claims for themselves.** Common forms of documentation include *footnotes* or *endnotes*.

• **Good critical writing avoids vague attributions.** *Vague attributions, as the term implies, attribute positions to sources without offering documented details*: "Virtually all Christians oppose abortions." "Most feminist philosophers favor abortion on demand."

Vague attributions can be an indication of inferior research. They do not provide support for an argument because they don't tell the reader enough. Precisely which Christians or feminists hold these views, if any? Are they important ones, or members of fringe groups? Further, by not clearly identifying their sources, vague attributions don't tell us how current their content is. To the discerning reader, vague attributions suggest sloppy, uncritical reasoning.

Vague attributions often signal bias and propaganda. Notice how Republican party candidates vaguely refer to "the Democrats" and how Democratic party candidates vaguely refer to "the Republicans." Different activist groups attribute offensive beliefs to "atheists," "secular humanists," "liberals," "fundamentalists," "white people," and so forth. Without specifying precisely who said exactly what, and in what context, claims supported by vague attributions function as propaganda, not evidence. Avoid sweeping, vague attributions. They never strengthen your case, and almost always weaken it.

• **Good critical writing avoids vague appeals to "common sense" or "common knowledge":** "Everybody knows . . . " "Decent people agree. . ." Such sweeping generalizations suffer from the same weaknesses as vague attributions. Further, they are virtually meaningless, since they are either obviously false (as in the first example), or contain loaded, unclear terms that substitute for evidence ("decent" in the second example).

• **Good critical writing is organized.** It contains an opening statement of the thesis or topic, a main body, and a clearly identified summation-conclusion. Every paragraph is relevant. The text moves toward a clearly defined goal.

FOUR GREAT WRITING TIPS

• *GREAT WRITING TIP NUMBER 1:* **Start writing right away, and plan on revising your finished paper at least once.**

• *GREAT WRITING TIP NUMBER 2: Look at* **your finished paper.** Are the paragraphs one sentence long? or one page long? If the paragraphs are uniformly long or short, the work may be poorly organized.

• *GREAT WRITING TIP NUMBER 3:* **Write the final version of the introduction and conclusion last.** Always match your introduction to your conclusion. A simple way to do this is to write only a tentative introduction to use as you develop your essay or paper. When you're finished with the body of the paper, word your conclusion in terms of what you've *actually shown*—and *then* write your final version of the introduction.

If you've shown A, B, C, and D, your conclusion might include something like: "In this essay I began by showing A. Having done that, I explained how B and C follow from A. This led to my main point, D."

After you've written the conclusion, write the final version of your introduction using key words and phrases from the conclusion. For example: "In this essay I begin by showing A. I next explain how B and C follow from A. This leads directly to my main point, D."

Framing your essay with a matching introduction and conclusion that *accurately describe* its content does three vital things: (1) It tells the reader what to expect. (2) It does what it promised to do. (3) It reminds the reader that it has done what it promised to do. Using key words and phrases in all three parts of the essay gives your work a polished coherence.

One of the saddest, avoidable errors writers make is not matching the introduction and conclusion with each other and with the body of the paper. If you begin with the announcement that you will show A, B, C, and D, and only show A, B, and C, you will have failed to substantiate your thesis. This is true even if D is a minor point.

Always double check the introduction and conclusion *after* you've finished the final version of the body of the paper. **CAUTION: This tip is not a substitute for good content. It will not obscure a weak effort.**

• *GREAT WRITING TIP NUMBER 4*: **Let your paper get "cold" before you make your last editing pass**. Set your paper aside long enough to develop some critical distance before you make your last revision. You will spot major and minor problems much easier if you can read your own work with a fresh eye—and a sufficient lapse of time is the best way to do this.

Form always matters, but it's not all that matters. In the last few years, I've noticed a tendency for some students to put more care into producing slick-looking papers—fancy titles, neat graphics, elegant paper, and such—than into producing substantive content. No doubt today's personal computers, high-quality printers, and powerful word processors make this tempting. Try to resist. And if you can't resist, at least make sure your paper's content has priority.

HOW TO PICK A TOPIC

• **Start thinking about possible topics as soon as the assignment is made.** Flag passages in the text that might make good topics—even if you're not personally interested in them. At this stage, you want as many ideas as possible. Ideas breed ideas. Jot down ideas, annoyances, or questions that provoke a response from you. Don't trust yourself to remember potential topics—write them down.

• **Think small.** One of the most common errors introductory philosophy students make in choosing a paper or essay topic is underestimating the amount of clarification and argumentation most critical writing requires. As a result, students sometimes pick huge topics that require writing a whole book.

> If you don't have much experience writing critically, follow this rule of thumb: If you think a topic is too small, it's probably about right. It's better to have "too much" evidence than not enough.

• **Word your topic precisely.** Vague topics tend to result in vague papers. Note the difference between these topics: "Existentialism" and "Sartre's Claim That We Choose the Advisor Most Likely to Tell Us What We Want to Hear." The second topic refers to a specific passage discussed in a textbook. The narrowness of the second topic is a virtue. It helps define and limit the writer's task. A general topic does not reflect an *idea*; it only indicates an *area*.

• **Don't take your topic *personally*.** You don't need to care about a subject to write well about it. Pick a topic that you can write well about in the amount of time you have. Be practical in your selection, considering what's going on in other courses you're taking, your job and family obligations, and your own actual work habits and abilities.

• **Forget about inspiration.** Don't fall into the trap of waiting for inspiration. Pick a topic as soon as you know the nature of the assignment. Waiting for inspiration may be a form of procrastination. Besides, inspiration may not come.

• **Unless you are an excellent critical writer, avoid defending your deepest personal beliefs.** For whatever reason, most of us are better at spotting weaknesses in ideas we dislike than we are at rationally supporting our own beliefs. A graded assignment in a philosophy class may not be the place to find out if you are an exception. Some of the poorest papers my colleagues and I receive are written in defense of the writer's most cherished beliefs. Their chief deficiency has been the substitution of heartfelt conviction and testimony for cogent argument and balanced documentation.

> Remember: There is no perfect topic. Don't make more out of your topic selection than you have to. Your paper is not your last and only chance to say something on this subject. Your topic needs to be relevant to the course, adequate in scope yet not overwhelming, and researchable given your current resources. That's all.

A QUICK GUIDE TO GETTING BETTER GRADES ON WRITING ASSIGNMENTS

• **Pick a topic early *and don't change it* (unless absolutely necessary).** Use the guidelines above to pick your topic. Then get right into it. Do any necessary research early. This will maximize the amount of time you have to process and refine your ideas.

• **Is instructor approval necessary? If so—obtain it.** Students sometimes overlook or omit this step.

• **Just write.** As soon as you have done your initial preparation (which may range from studying a portion of your textbook to library research), write something. Write quickly, ignoring—for the moment—organization, grammar, and spelling. See where your mind wants to go. The very act of writing enhances the critical thinking process.

• **Form a semi-rough draft.** Once you've written a rough draft, you're ready to give it a more polished form. Shape paragraphs, move ideas around, elaborate, explain, clarify.

• **Define all key terms when you introduce them.** Be sure to specify exactly how you are using any key technical terms. *Do not use a conventional dictionary to define technical philosophical terms.* Conventional dictionaries only provide common, socially correct usage. Doctors and lawyers use medical and legal dictionaries, and you should use a good *philosophical dictionary*, primary sources, references like the *Encyclopedia of Philosophy* (see bibliography), and your textbook to define key philosophical terms.

• **After you have written your first complete polished version, put it away and forget about it.** Let your work get cold. You'll need time to do this. That's why you picked a topic quickly and got to work early. Set the paper aside for a day or two at least—a week is better. This will help you acquire the critical distance you'll need to take an objective look at your work.

• **Critically revise.** Once you've established "critical distance" by setting your paper aside for a time, you're ready for careful revision. Read your paper as if you were grading it. Mark it up. As you read, ask yourself: Is the thesis clearly stated? Does each step lead logically to what follows? Are important points supported with clearly stated reasons? Are terms used consistently? Are claims supported with documented sources, as needed? Does the paper make its case? Improve the text as you answer these questions *with your thesis clearly in mind.*

• **If necessary, modify your original thesis.** Once they have begun work on a topic, it's common for philosophical writers to discover that their original plan can be improved by selective modification. Perhaps too much is included, so some pruning is in order. Or perhaps what originally looked like a minor point has turned out to be crucial, so shifting and beefing up are in order. The point is, writing is not like captaining a ship. You're not honor bound to go down with a leaky vessel. Abandon a shaky topic, if it can't be salvaged. Sometimes, there's no way to know that topic won't work for you until you have a go at it. (But this should be a last resort. That's why picking a topic is so important.)

• **Don't be seduced by computerized spell-checkers and grammar-checkers.** Spell-checkers don't always contain technical philosophical terms. Spell-checking cannot catch the misuse of homonyms (words that sound alike) such as "two," "to," or "too." They may not catch correctly spelled but entirely inappropriate words. They don't catch omissions or redundancies. Different grammar-checkers have different protocols. None of them is entirely foolproof. You need to proofread your work even if you use these aides. To see why, study the anonymous poem that pops up on electronic bulletin boards:

> I have a spelling checker,
> It came with my PC;
> It plainly marks four my revue
> Mistakes I cannot sea.
> I've run this pome threw it,
> I'm sure your pleased to no,
> It's letter perfect in its weigh,
> My checker tolled me sew.
> I only rote it one thyme,
> Two let you here it rhyme,
> Bee for I drank sum tee,
> And inn my bed eye clime.

• **Don't confuse a good-looking, properly spelled, grammatically correct paper with a good paper.** Your professor has a right to *expect* a neat, grammatical paper. That's the minimum in philosophy classes, not the maximum. The mechanics of your paper should be "transparent," unnoticed by the reader. A mechanically correct paper allows its content to shine forth. Your philosophy professor may or may not mark grammatical errors, but he or she will certainly note them—and they will almost certainly damage the critical content of your writing.

• **Stop when you've made your point.** Don't pad your paper. Few philosophy instructors are impressed by sheer volume. You're probably better off saying less very precisely and coherently, than saying more sloppily. As with all advice, make sure this suggestion applies to your circumstances. If your instructor places a premium on length, then pick your topic accordingly. You're still going to need to be clear and precise, however, no matter how long your paper is. Even if you have to write a long paper—don't pad it.

- **Document *all* sources.** *Plagiarism occurs when you use someone else's exact words (or a close paraphrase) without giving them credit.* Plagiarism is one of the most serious academic "sins."

Plagiarism in the form of *excessive paraphrasing* is unusually easy to spot as the writing style of the text keeps shifting, and the content of some passages is too sophisticated for introductory-level work.

If you find that you are going back and forth between reading and writing, always consulting your text, you are in danger of excessive paraphrasing. Your best safeguard is to use separate note cards to jot down all key quotations and brief summaries of key ideas. Organize your cards, and then write in your own words, inserting carefully selected and cited quotes.

Any time you are using someone else's idea without significant modification, you need to document its originator.

You have nothing to lose by citing good sources, and a great deal to lose by plagiarizing them, since penalties range from flunking an assignment to expulsion from college.

> Ironically, not citing sources almost always results in a poorer grade than crediting sources would have, because citing authorities and experts of established reputation adds their expertise and authority to your own excellent ideas. When you don't give credit to established experts, you deprive your paper of important support.

- **Follow instructions.** Let's admit it. Many of the requirements instructors insist on are just their preferences. In the great scheme of things, who cares whether you use staples or paper clips, plastic covers or title sheets? *The person grading your work cares, that's who!* And that's a pretty good reason to follow instructions. It may not matter in the grand scheme of things whether you use footnotes, endnotes, or in-text citations. If, however, your *instructor*

says endnotes, it matters to your grade. Use whatever style guide or manual your instructor requires. If none is specified, ask for guidance. Use the kind of paper, binder, and ink specified. Follow instructions regarding title pages and paper clips, margins, bibliographies, type-size, spacing, and due dates. If your instructor has not specified these things, *ASK*. Don't assume. Get clear information right away.

• **Use a good dictionary and approved style guide.** Simply assume that spelling and grammar count—don't embarrass yourself by asking. Consult your instructor regarding preferred style guidelines. (See the Beginning Philosopher's Bibliography at the back of this book for the names of some good style guides.)

• **Type your work.** Other things being equal, neatly typed assignments get higher grades than handwritten ones. Take advantage of this. (But neat garbage is still garbage, and neatly typed garbage is a waste of everybody's time.)

• **Stick to the length specified.** Unless explicitly told otherwise, use conventional margins, double spacing, and use 10- or 12-point font if you have a word processor. Play fair. Don't try to pad a thin paper with huge printing and exaggerated margins, and don't exceed length requirements with small print, small margins, and space-and-a-half printing. To be safe, try to get a specified word count rather than page length.

• **Proofread your final draft.** It is much better to make one or two neat corrections by hand than to ignore typos, spelling errors, bad grammar, gross inconsistencies. If you have more than two corrections on a page, redo it. *This is another reason to allow plenty of time for the entire writing process, from topic selection to typing or printing the final version.*

• **Keep at least one copy of your paper in a safe place.** Your instructor is not the one who will suffer if your paper is lost or damaged.

• **Turn in the original or a high quality photocopy, not a faint, smudged, or black-edged photocopy.**

• **Use a good ribbon or printer, and do not use onion skin, easy-erase, or colored paper.**

• **Plan ahead to get to school early on the due date.** Some instructors penalize late papers. Allow for possible transportation problems and other contingencies.

• **If you need special consideration, talk to your instructor as soon as you are aware of special needs.** Don't be embarrassed to request special consideration, if you really need it. On the other hand, don't think of just being busy or apprehensive about writing a paper as a special need. Most students are very busy, and at least moderately nervous, about turning in written work.

• **Always study your graded paper.** Try to understand why your instructor gave you that grade. If you need more explanation than is provided with the graded paper, politely request it.

• **Cool off before you decide you were cheated on your grade.** If you feel that your grade is inaccurate, *after setting the paper aside for a few days and carefully rereading it*, courteously request a rereading by your instructor.

• **If your instructor does not return graded papers, make an appointment to review and discuss your paper during office hours.** If you plan to discuss your paper with the instructor, be sure to give him or her time to review it before the discussion.

FOUR WRITING SAMPLES FOR YOU TO GRADE

Next to writing experience, perhaps the best way to improve your critical writing is by reading other people's critical writing. In some writing courses, students exchange essays and rough drafts of papers for the purpose of offering positive criticism. They help one another identify strengths and weaknesses, and get a better idea of how good writing differs from poor writing.

The following essays were written by students in an introduction to philosophy course. The essays were written in class as part of an announced closed-book test. Two weeks before the test, the instructor distributed a list of questions from which the actual test question would be selected. The review questions all referred to specific topics covered in Chapter 12 of the textbook *Archetypes of Wisdom: An Introduction to Philosophy,* Third Edition. Sartre's claim that "existence precedes essence" was discussed at length in class, as well. The students were asked: **What did Sartre mean by the phrase "existence precedes essence?" Why is the issue important? Do you agree with Sartre? Explain?**

As you read each of the unedited essays, use these questions as guidelines for your evaluation. See if you think the essays clearly and directly answer the question.

- Would an intelligent reader who is *unfamiliar* with Sartre's idea get a clear introduction to its meaning from the essay?

- Does the essay give evidence of familiarity with the assigned readings? For instance, does it use specific examples or concepts from the text?

- Are the sentences grammatically correct and is the essay well organized (given the time constraints of an in-class essay)?

- Based on your answers to these questions, what grade would you give each essay? Why?

Note: It's a good idea to read all four essays before assigning grades to any of them.

SAMPLE ESSAY 1
What did Sartre mean by the phrase "existence precedes essence?" Why is the issue important? Do you agree with Sartre? Explain?

He means that you first must be a human on this earth before you have an essence. This is important because if you are not in existence then how can there be essence. Existence is very important. I agree with this because I also feel that there must be existence before essence. This is important for humans as well as others. Sartre had his own ways and so do many others, of everything.

SAMPLE ESSAY 2
What did Sartre mean by the phrase "existence precedes essence?" Why is the issue important? Do you agree with Sartre? Explain?

Sartre meant that you as a person are not born a certain way. Nobody is born a coward or is born a bad person. The person has control over their own actions and if they <u>choose</u> to be brave they will do brave things just as if they only committed cowardly acts they would be cowards but by choice. This is important because if it were true then a person could not excuse behavior such as robbery or murder just because they had a bad childhood or they were in a violent neighborhood and couldn't help it. I agree with Sartre. To me you always have a choice and I think that making excuses like the ones above are a "cop-out". Even if you decide not to choose between two evils you still have made a choice. There is always a choice and we have free will.

SAMPLE ESSAY 3
**What did Sartre mean by the phrase "existence precedes essence?"
Why is the issue important? Do you agree with Sartre? Explain?**

Existence precedes essence means that "you are fundamentally what you do." You are your actions. There is no "essence" that you are born with. Your actions shape you and make you what you are. You must decide upon your actions and be responsible for them. You are free to choose but must face the consequences they bring. I agree with Sartre.

SAMPLE ESSAY 4
**What did Sartre mean by the phrase "existence precedes essence?"
Why is the issue important? Do you agree with Sartre? Explain?**

What Sartre meant by existence precedes essence is that our actions and choices develop our values. In a simpler manner, what we do is what we are. People are not born with certain values. They make choices and act in the value spectrum they choose.

Sartre said "Consciousness has incalculable consequences." He did not like the excuse that I can do something bad because not everybody does it. He said to choose with our eyes open and with responsibility. Sartre's idea was in contrast to Kant's philosophy of motives. Sartre said we are condemned to be free because there is no God. So everything is permitted.

I agree sort of. I do not agree about God. I believe in God. But I do think what we do is more important than what we think. I do not like excuses. But sometimes I think people can't help what they do. So I guess I think existence precedes essence most of the time. But some people, babies and brain damaged people, are not free. So how can they be condemned to be free?

A LAST LOOK AT THE FOUR SAMPLE ESSAYS

You're probably wondering what grades the four sample essays got in "real life."

• **Sample Essay 1 received an F.** It is much too general, and most of what it does say is confusing. *Nothing* in the essay indicates familiarity with the assigned readings. The essay is too short, and repeats what little it does say. The sentence "I agree with this because I also feel that there must be existence before essence," is a form of a fallacy known as *begging the question*. **Begging the question occurs when an argument uses some form of its conclusion as evidence for that very conclusion.** In this case, the author of the essay has really said nothing more than: *I agree with Sartre because I agree with him.*

• **Sample Essay 2 received a B+.** By opening with the example of being born a coward, the author of Sample Essay 2 signals the reader that he or she is familiar with the assignment. The author then proceeds to develop the idea, using the concepts of choice and excuse making. This at least implies recognition of the importance of responsibility to Sartre. The closing reference to free will indicates awareness of another important, related issue. Compare this essay's fuller statement to the begged question that concludes Sample Essay 1: "I agree with Sartre. To me you always have a choice and I think that making excuses like the ones above are a 'cop-out.' Even if you decide not to choose between two evils you still have made a choice. There is always a choice and we have free will."

• **Sample Essay 3 received a C-.** This essay is clear, and what it does say is *generally correct*. But it is also repetitive. Worse, the essay does not make it clear that the author studied the assigned reading. That's a big problem with "generally okay." essays. Further, the writer merely *states* "I agree with Sartre," without offering any *explanation*, as is called for in the instructions. A cynical reader could interpret this essay as being *evasive*. That is, the lack of specific examples from the assigned readings, combined with the repetition, could be interpreted as evidence of failure to read the assignment thoroughly, or at all. A more charitable reader might *assume* that the writer knew more than he or she said, and attribute the essay's weaknesses to lack of writing experience. The essay is weak because it is ambiguous and vague.

• **Sample Essay 4 received an A-.** This essay contains multiple references to the assigned readings, making it very clear that its author had studied them. Although overall the essay is clear, the last two sentences in the first paragraph are not: "People are not born with certain values. They make choices and act in the value spectrum they choose." Whatever this writer meant needed clarification. The statement "Sartre said 'Consciousness has incalculable consequences.'" is not entirely correct. Sartre did not *say* that in so many words. The student is confusing a characterization of Sartre's ideas by the textbook's author with Sartre's own words. But this kind of "error" on an in-class, closed-book test is trivial. The essay makes it clear that this student did the assignment, even going so far as to memorize what he or she recognized as an important point. Finally, compare this writer's explanation of why he or she agrees with Sartre with the closing remarks in the other three essays. This writer's explanation is the most sophisticated of the four because it is a *qualified* agreement, accepting some of Sartre's ideas, but not all of them—and offering examples to support the writer's point of view: "I agree sort of. I do not agree about God. I believe in God. But I do think what we do is more important than what we think. I do not like excuses. But sometimes I think people can't help what they do. So I guess I think existence precedes essence most of the time. But some people, babies and brain damaged people, are not free. So how can they be condemned to be free?"

How did your grades compare with each essay's actual grades?

CHARACTERISTICS OF GOOD AND BAD ESSAYS

Many students think that essay assignments and tests are "subjective" in the sense that they have no one "right answer." Perhaps you've had the common experience of being absolutely convinced that you were cheated on an essay assignment because you wrote "the same thing" as your friend who got a better grade. This may be correct in some sense, but remember that no matter how similar two essays are, they are not *exactly the same*. Grades can be affected by the order in which topics are covered, word choice, organization (paragraphing), sentence structure, nature and number of examples, degree of specificity, and so forth. Your essay may be very similar to your friend's, but your professor is probably responding to the *whole essay effect*, as well as to individual aspects that your essay may share with your friend's.

Does this mean that essay grades are subjective in the sense of being capricious or arbitrarily relative? In fact, there is a high degree of consistency among grading standards of experienced professors. Professor W may be slightly tougher than Professor Y, so that a B+ from Professor W is roughly equivalent to an A from Professor Y, but the *relative rankings* of their grades will tend to conform. That means that it is highly unlikely that an essay that gets an A from Professor Y would get a D or an F from Professor W.

In doing the research for this book, I have identified certain common characteristics that affect the way many professors grade essays. Knowing what these are can help you write better essays and papers (since essays and papers share many fundamental features). Here's what I found, which, incidentally, reaffirmed my own grading practices.

- **Spelling and grammar should always matter.** Having a grammatically correct essay cannot substitute for not knowing the material, but poor grammar and spelling detract from even the best ideas.

- **Length matters, but not in a simplistic way.** Essays that call for explanation, elaboration, or critical evaluation must be long enough to cover everything asked for. Past that point, however, length is not a reliable indicator of quality. A lot of irrelevant, unclear, or incorrect material only underscores lack of preparation. Avoid padding your essays.

- **Good essays answer the question as it is asked.** This is just another form of following instructions, which is always fundamental. Writing brilliantly about something else, even something closely related to the assignment, is not a substitute for showing your professor that you understand the specific material he or she wants to test you on.

- **Good essays offer reasonable, relevant, sufficient evidence to support their claims.** Poor essays tend to settle for merely making assertions, or offering vague or sweeping statements as support.

- **Good essays are specific.** Good essays use precise, correct terms and examples from assigned readings. Good essays refer to individuals by name on a regular basis. Poor essays use "he," "she," or "they" too often.

- **Good essays make it very clear that their writers are familiar with *both* assigned readings *and* lectures *and* class discussions.** This is another way of being specific, rather than general and vague.

- **Good essays reflect organized thought.** Good take-home essays are well structured and organized. Sufficiently well organized in-class essays indicate careful studying and planning. Jumbled, chaotic take-home essays imply lack of preparation and effort. Jumbled, chaotic in-class essays are more difficult to interpret, but assuming that you have the prerequisite language skills for a philosophy class, poorly organized work suggests lack of preparation.

- **Excellent essays provide unique examples and explanations.** Excellent essays reflect a solid grasp of the material, but in their own unique voice. They do not just repeat examples and explanations from the text and lectures.

- **Excellent essays draw conclusions and make inferences that go beyond class material.** These can be in the form of questions, criticisms, identification of inconsistencies, and so forth.

- **Essays decline in quality with each of the following avoidable weaknesses:**

√ **Misspelled names and key terms:** This implies that you have not read the material at all, or that you have not studied it carefully. At the very least, you should identify all key figures and technical terms, and memorize their correct spellings.

√   **Factual errors:** Factual errors include attributing ideas to the wrong source, or distorting a philosopher's views.

√   **Irrelevant material:** Weak essays rely on irrelevant personal comments and anecdotes ("I had a lot of trouble picking a topic. At first I was going to write about Plato . . ."), or distracting analyses of concepts that do not directly answer the question as it is framed.

√   **Unexplained or unsupported key assertions:** The last sentence in Sample Essay 3 is a classic example of this error. Repeating the same point in different words is a common variant of this mistake, since merely asserting something more than once does not somehow become evidence for its truth.

√   **Merely listing lots of ideas:** Students who receive lower grades than they were expecting sometimes express considerable frustration when they feel that they have "included everything you said was important." Including all important material is only a *necessary step* in writing a good analytic or critical essay, however. But because a critical essay is different from a summary or report, a mere "laundry list" approach is not *sufficient*. A list or summary is never a substitute for a cogent analysis.

√   **Numerous mechanical errors:** At the very least, numerous errors indicate that the writer has not proofread his or her work. More seriously, numerous basic errors of grammar can identify a need for remedial writing courses; this is always a disappointment, but not something the motivated college student can avoid dealing with.

A SIMPLIFIED STYLE GUIDE FOR
EXCELLENT PAPERS

Here's a simplified style guide that should be sufficient for most introductory-level philosophy papers and essays. It's based on the fourth edition of Joseph Gibaldi's *MLA Handbook for Writers of Research Papers*. Before you use any style guide check with your instructor.

•   **Handwritten papers:** Standard size (8 1/2 x 11 inches), wide-lined notebook paper. Use black or dark blue ink. Write on one side of the page. Do not use sheets torn out of a spiral-bound notebook.

•   **Typed papers and essays:** Standard size (8 1/2 x 11 inches), heavy paper. Do not use onionskin or easy-erase paper; they smudge. Use a good, black ribbon or printer with plenty of ink or toner.

•   **Double-space all text.** Skip every other ruled line for handwritten papers.

•   **Use only one side of the page.**

•   **Do not use fancy type.** Use a conventional (Roman) typeface. Do not use script or italics for the body of your text. Use italics (or underline) for titles, or when quoting italicized material. In formal academic writing, you should probably avoid italics, boldface, and exclamation points. Let the power and quality of your writing provide the emphasis you want to convey.

•   **Word processors:** Same as typed plus: 10- or 12-point font. Avoid excessive use of graphics and fancy print styles. Concentrate on content. The printer should be set on highest quality (not draft) mode. Do not right-justify or center the body of your text.

•   **Margins:** One inch, top, bottom, and both sides. (Use the ruled margin lines provided on most lined notebook paper.)

•   **Name and course information:** You do not need a title page for a research paper or essay. Put your name one inch from the top and flush with the *left* margin *on the first page* of your paper or essay. Under your name and on separate, double-spaced lines, type your instructor's name, the course name and number, and the date, flush with the left margin.

• **Title:** Center the title one double-spaced line down from the date. Double-space between the title and the first line of text. Do not underline or put quotation marks around your title. You should, however, underline any words in the title that you would underline elsewhere in the text, such as titles. For example, if you were writing about Descartes' *Meditations*, You need to underline Meditations because that is the title of the book you are writing about. The first lines of the first page of your essay would look something like this:

Ima Happy

Professor Wyse

Introduction to Philosophy 101

August 14, 1997

An Analysis of Descarte's Meditations

In this essay I will show that Cartesian dualism is

inconsistent with the experiences of most people. First, I

will show

• **Page numbers:** Do not number the title page. Beginning with page two, number all pages consecutively; upper right-hand corner, one-half inch from the top and flush with the right margin. Type only your last name before each page number. Leave one or two spaces between your name and the page number. Use Arabic numerals (1, 2, 3, etc.). Do not use *p* as an abbreviation for "page," and do not use a hyphen, period, or any other mark or symbol. Here's a sample page 2:

Pesavento 2

and consequently and induitably I have established that

• **Paragraphs:** Indent the first line of all paragraphs five spaces or one-half inch. Double space as usual between paragraphs—do not leave extra space.

• **Extended Quotations:** If a quote runs more than three lines, indent the entire quote ten spaces (or one inch) from the left margin, and cite your source. If it runs less than three lines, embed it in the text (don't forget quotation marks), and cite your source.

• **Fasteners:** Unless your instructor tells you otherwise, staple or paper clip your paper together in the upper left hand corner, after checking to see which, if either, your professor prefers. Do not use binders or covers, since a stack of them can be cumbersome for instructors to cart around, and they can make it difficult to write editorial comments on your paper. Never, ever use the old "pinch, tear, and fold" method—unless *specifically instructed* to do so.

• **Corrections and insertions:** *Always* proofread your work carefully in time to make corrections. If you are using a word processor, correct the mistake and then reprint the entire page. If you are not using a word processor—and if your instructor allows—insert brief, neatly printed corrections immediately above the error using a caret (∧). Do not use margins to make corrections. Do not make corrections below the lines. Never make more than one or two small corrections per page, and never make corrections on more than two pages of papers less than four pages long. Consult your instructor regarding longer papers.

• **Do not expect your instructor, or the college, to provide you with staples, paper clips, binders, and such:** It is your responsibility to have your paper completely finished and ready to hand in by the date and time your instructor specifies.

• **If you are planning to use the college's computer or writing lab to write your paper, check out lab schedules and computer availability right away:** If necessary, sign up for ample computer time. Budget time for emergencies and down time.

• **If you are hiring a typist, allow plenty of time to proofread, and, if necessary, retype the final draft:** Be very clear with the typist regarding how much time he or she will need, and so forth. Begin lining up a good typist early, and stay in touch once you find one. *Remember that no matter who helps you type your paper, you are the one responsible for fulfilling all requirements—and you're the one getting graded.*

• **If you are using a word processor, save, save, save, and back up, back up, back up.** Save your work regularly as you type, and always keep two sets of your files—a working disk and a backup disk. It's also a good idea to give a different name to each draft or version of your work-in-progress. One way to do this is to use the date (Plato 8.14.97) or a sequential alpha or numeric suffix (Plato1, Plato 2, PlatoA, PlatoB). Never work on your only copy of a file. If possible keep copies of your disks in separate places.

CITATIONS

Acknowledge *all* direct quotes and paraphrases of others' ideas by keying brief parenthetical citations in your text to an alphabetical list of works cited that follows the text. Citations allow scholars and interested readers to verify your research, to get additional information, or to build upon your work. Scrupulous citing is a hallmark of ethical and competent scholarship. Be sure, then, to cite all sources in such a way that a curious reader could, if she or he wished, consult them directly. To that end, scholars follow certain conventions (stylistic arrangements) for documenting source material. The three most common are MLA (Modern Language Association), APA (American Psychological Association), and Chicago Manual of Style (Chicago or Turabian, after Kate L. Turabian). MLA and Chicago are widely used in many areas of specialization. APA is favored for scientifically oriented articles. Check to see if your instructor prefers one of these, or another, citation format. Whatever format you use, be sure to include: Author. Title. Publication Information. Date.

• **In-text citations:** Increasingly, scholars are using in-text citations rather than endnotes or footnotes for essays and research papers, for modest works, or work aimed at general audiences, although endnotes and footnotes are also still widely used. Be sure to check with *each* of your instructors to see which format is required for each of your courses.

The elegance and ease of using the in-text format make it especially appealing to writers who do not have access to word processing programs. (Typing footnotes can be quite a task, particularly for the novice or infrequent typist.)

The following overview of the in-text citation format provides enough detail for most undergraduate philosophy writing assignments. You will note that minimal information is given in the in-text citation. You will provide complete bibliographic information in a list of works cited, which will be explained below. If your work is more sophisticated, your library and bookstore should have a selection of helpful style and research guides.

As a rule, in-text citations following the popular MLA format only include the author's last name and page number in the text (Fetters 123). If you are presenting time-sensitive scientific research, the date should be noted as part of the parenthetical in-text citation (Vargas, 1997, p. 88). The Fetters example conforms to MLA (Modern Language Association) style and the Vargas example conforms to APA (American Psychological Association) style for books.

When citing sources that do not indicate who the author is, substitute a short version of the title containing a key word or two. If two or more authors have the same last name, use first initials.

Be sure to document *all* quotations and paraphrases. Unless instructed otherwise, you should be safe using the modified MLA format described in this chapter. The information you use—author's name, shortened titles, and such—is determined by your list of works cited.

Always make sure that you understand *exactly* what format your instructor requires or prefers as soon as you are given any writing assignment. And then follow that format.

CONSTRUCTING A LIST OF WORKS CITED

Title your list <u>Works Cited</u>, and place it, beginning as a separate, numbered page, at the end of your paper. Center the title—<u>Works Cited</u>—one inch from the top of the page. Double-space the entire works cited. The first line of each citation is put flush with the left margin. Indent the second and subsequent lines five spaces or one-half inch. Include all sources: books, articles, online sources, films, CD-ROM sources, and television and radio sources. Proper punctuation is provided in the illustrative examples that follow.

• **Titles:** <u>Underline</u> the titles of books. Put magazine and journal article titles in "quotation" marks. Underline all book, pamphlet, periodical, CD-ROM and diskette titles. Treat individual articles from CD-ROM and diskette sources like magazine and journal article titles by setting them off in quotation marks.

• **Cities:** You do not need to list states or countries for such well known cities as London, Chicago, San Francisco, Bolivia, or Paris. You do need to list states or countries for lesser known cities: Belmont, Ca., Herkimer, N.Y., Brunswick, Mo. When two or more cities share the same name, give additional information for the less well known: Cairo, Il., Paris, Tx. When two or more cities are equally well known, give additional information for each: Cambridge, Eng., Cambridge, Ma.

- **Books by one author:** Author's name, last name first. Book Title. City of publisher: Publisher, date. Identify translators or editors after the title. Examples:

Jaspers, Karl. Socrates, Buddha, Confucius, Jesus: The

Paradigmatic Individuals, ed. Hannah Arendt, trans. Ralph

Manheim. New York: Harcourt Brace Jovanovich, 1962.

- **Books by two or more authors:** List each author in the order they appear on the title page; reverse the first and last name of the first author only. Example:

Kolak, Daniel, and Raymond Martin, The Experience of

Philosophy. Belmont, Ca.: Wadsworth Publishing Company,

1990.

- **Two or more books by the same author:** Give the name for the first entry only. Use three hyphens followed by a period and the title for all subsequent entries (three hyphens stand for exactly the same name as the name for the preceding entry.) Examples:

Soccio, Douglas. Archetypes of Wisdom: An Introduction to

Philosophy, Third Edition. Belmont, Ca.: Wadsworth

Publishing Company, 1998.

---. How to Get the Most Out of Philosophy, Third Edition.

Belmont, Ca.: Wadsworth Publishing Company, 1998.

---, and Vincent E. Barry. Practical Logic: An Antidote to

Uncritical Thinking, Fifth Edition. Fort Worth, Tx.:

Harcourt Brace, 1998.

- **Books by corporate authors:** Commissions, associations, committees, and any other group whose individual members are not identified are treated as "corporate authors." (Sometimes, the publisher is also the corporate author.) Example:

American Medical Association. The American Medical

    Association Encyclopedia of Medicine. New York: Random

    House, 1989.

- **Articles in periodicals:** Author. "Article Title." Magazine or
Journal Title volume number (date): inclusive page numbers.
    For newspapers: Author. "Article Title." Newspaper name as
it appears on the masthead Date Month Year: Page(s). If the name
of the city, is not given for a local paper, insert it after the name in
square brackets [ ], but don't underline it. If the newspaper prints
more than one edition (early, late, national, and such), add a
comma after the date and give the edition.
    Abbreviate the names of every month except May, June, and
July. If the paper contains sections (A, B, C, D), include them as
part of the first page number. Here are some examples of
periodical sources:

Borst, Missy. "Teaching Is My Life." California Bugle [Fillmore]

    20 Feb. 1971: D6-9.

Gilmar, Sybil T. "Language Foreign to U. S. School," Editorial.

    Philadelphia Inquirer 25 Apr. 1990: A17.

Joelson, J. R. "English: The Language of Liberty." The Humanist

    July/Aug (1989): 35-38.

Linville, George-Janet. "What Ever Became of Human Nature?"

    Computers and the Social Sciences 14 (1996): 118-123.

Malone, Midgetta. "Crediting the Amanuensis: When

    Proofreading Becomes an Act of Creation." Riverside

    Philophaster 11 Aug. 1989, natl. ed.: A1.

Cooney, Kenneth Rian. "Make English the Official Language,"

    Letter. Chicago Tribune (August 30, 1997) sec. 4: 2.

• **CD-ROMS, diskettes, and magnetic tapes:** CD-ROMS, diskettes, and magnetic tapes are sometimes referred to as portable databases for the obvious reason that they can be easily transported and consulted. When citing portable databases be sure to identify the *publication medium* (CD-ROM, diskette, magnetic tape), the *vendor's name, and the date of electronic publication.* This information is necessary because there may be different versions of a data source, each with the same title. Because there are so many different configurations of portable databases, you should consult your instructor or a more complete style guide if you are unfamiliar with this form of citation. Examples:

American Heritage Dictionary. Microsoft Bookshelf. 1993 ed.

   CD-ROM. Redmond, Wa.: Microsoft, 1993.

Carter, J. Scott. "Truman's Legacy of Responsibility." Carter's

   PoliSci DataSource. Magnetic tape. Trinity, Ca.: Serfdom,

   1996.

CIA World Factbook. CD-ROM. Minneapolis: Quanta, 1992.

Hinshaw, Carl Rogers. Stress: The Student's Friend. Vers. 1a.

   Diskette. Clarence Psychological Resources, 1995.

Oxford English Dictionary. 2nd, Ed. CD-ROM. Oxford: Oxford

   University Press, 1992.

Where in the World is Carmen Sandiego? Deluxe ed. CD-ROM.

   Novato, Ca.: Brøderbund, 1992.

• **Online sources:** Online data bases are "intangible" in the sense that you cannot buy them, store them, or carry them with you. They are often large, and regularly modified and updated. It can be difficult, if not impossible, to be sure that the material available at a given time is the same as it was when previously consulted. Consequently, data from online sources requires careful scrutiny (as, of course, do all sources). Also, online data is considered "published," or unique, whenever it is posted or modified.

Thus, online citations must always include the publication medium, computer service or network, and access date.

Publication medium. Identify your source medium as Online.

Name of computer service or network. Dialog, CompuServe, Prodigy are examples of computer services. The Internet is a vast computer network; as such, it is inadequate as a citation source without other information, so be sure to provide the name of the server or website address of your source.)

Access date. Because each online "publication" is considered unique, you may have to list more than one date, particularly if you are citing a source originally published in another medium, such as a magazine or newspaper. A complete citation will include the hard copy date and the online date.

Examples of online source citations:

Alston, Robin. "The Battle of the Books." Humanist 7.0176 (10

Sept. 1993): 10 pp. Online. Internet. 10 Oct. 1993.

"Middle Ages." Academic American Encyclopedia. Online.

Prodigy. 30 Mar. 1992.

Shakespeare, William. Hamlet. The Works of William

Shakespeare. Ed. Arthur H. Bullen. Stratford Town Ed.

Stratford-on-Avon: Shakespeare Head, 1911. Online.

Dartmouth College Library. Internet. 26 Dec. 1992.

CAUTION: This is a *simplified* style guide. Be sure your instructor approves of its use. And make an investment in your education by purchasing your own copy of a good style guide. Ask your instructors for recommendations or see the Bibliography at the end of this book.

A SAMPLE WORKS CITED

This sample contains all of the preceding examples, arranged alphabetically.

Works Cited

Alston, Robin. "The Battle of the Books." Humanist 7.0176 (10 Sept. 1993): 10 pp. Online. Internet. 10 Oct. 1993.

American Heritage Dictionary. Microsoft Bookshelf. 1993 ed. CD-ROM. Redmond, Wa.: Microsoft, 1993.

American Medical Association. The American Medical Association Encyclopedia of Medicine. New York: Random House, 1989.

Borst, Missy. "Teaching Is My Life." California Bugle [Fillmore] 20 Feb. 1971: D6-9.

Carter, J. Scott. "Truman's Legacy of Responsibility." Carter's PoliSci DataSource. Magnetic tape. Trinity, Ca.: Serfdom, 1996.

CIA World Factbook. CD-ROM. Minneapolis: Quanta, 1992.

Cooney, Kenneth Rian. "Make English the Official Language," Letter. Chicago Tribune (August 30, 1997) sec. 4: 2.

Gilmar, Sybil T. "Language Foreign to U. S. School," Editorial. Philadelphia Inquirer 25 Apr. 1990: A17.

Hinshaw, Carl Rogers. Stress: The Student's Friend. Vers. 1a. Diskette. Clarence Psychological Resources, 1995.

Jaspers, Karl. Socrates, Buddha, Confucius, Jesus: The Paradigmatic Individuals, ed. Hannah Arendt, trans. Ralph Manheim. New York: Harcourt Brace Jovanovich, 1962.

Joelson, J. R. "English: The Language of Liberty." The Humanist July/Aug (1989): 35-38.

Kolak, Daniel, and Raymond Martin, The Experience of
    Philosophy. Belmont, Ca.: Wadsworth Publishing Company,
    1990.

Linville, George-Janet. "What Ever Became of Human Nature?"
    Computers and the Social Sciences 14 (1996): 118-123.

Malone, Midgetta. "Crediting the Amanuensis: When
    Proofreading Becomes an Act of Creation." Riverside
    Philophaster 11 Aug. 1989, natl. ed.: A1.

"Middle Ages." Academic American Encyclopedia. Online.
    Prodigy. 30 Mar. 1992.

Oxford English Dictionary. 2nd, Ed. CD-ROM. Oxford: Oxford
    University Press, 1992.

Shakespeare, William. Hamlet. The Works of William
    Shakespeare. Ed. Arthur H. Bullen. Stratford Town Ed.
    Stratford-on-Avon: Shakespeare Head, 1911. Online.
    Dartmouth College Library. Internet. 26 Dec. 1992.

Soccio, Douglas. Archetypes of Wisdom: An Introduction to
    Philosophy, Third Edition. Belmont, Ca.: Wadsworth
    Publishing Company, 1998.

---. How to Get the Most Out of Philosophy, Third Edition.
    Belmont, Ca.: Wadsworth Publishing Company, 1998.

---, and Vincent E. Barry. Practical Logic: An Antidote to
    Uncritical Thinking, Fifth Edition. Fort Worth, Tx.:
    Harcourt Brace, 1998.

Where in the World is Carmen Sandiego? Deluxe ed. CD-ROM.
    Novato, Ca.: Brøderbund, 1992.

A HANDY CHECKLIST FOR
BETTER CRITICAL WRITING

Review this list whenever you write, proofread, or revise.

_____ Is the first paragraph so clear that any reader will know exactly what the topic is?

_____ Does the first or second paragraph clearly describe your strategy for dealing with your topic?

_____ Are all sentences grammatically correct?

_____ Are all sentences punctuated correctly?

_____ Are all technical terms spelled correctly?

_____ Is your essay or paper well organized?

_____ Does your essay or paper use specific examples and language to show that you are familiar with the assigned readings and any other important material?

_____ Does your essay or paper end with a clear and obvious summtion and conclusion, keyed precisely and directly to what you say in the body of the text?

_____ Are your topic and conclusion paragraphs consistent?

_____ Does your paper have a complete, properly formatted (and punctuated) list of works cited?

_____ Have you followed all formatting instructions discussed in A Simplified Style Guide For Excellent Papers (or the guide required by your instructor)?

_____ Are all sources properly documented?

_____ Have you proofread the final version of your essay or paper?

A BRIEF NOTE ABOUT THE INTERNET

Like so many other things, the Internet's strengths are also its weaknesses. These include virtually unlimited freedom of expression, communication, and access. But this very openness and availability requires caution when we turn to "the Internet" for information and advice. The ease with which individuals and groups can establish websites or "publish" information via newsrooms, chat rooms, intranets, e-mail, and the like, allows virtually anyone to claim virtually anything.

Conventionally, works published in academic, scientific, and technical fields have had to "pass muster" by "blind peer reviewing." Thus, an article published in the American Philosophical Quarterly can be assumed to have "competed" with other candidates for publication by being evaluated by professional philosophers specializing in the areas discussed in the candidate articles. Ideally, this assures that certain standards are met, and that the article knows whereof it speaks. In the sciences, peer review and publication of experimental protocols and data reinforce basic principles of scientific method: Verification or rejection by disinterested—even hostile—peers.

The rapid proliferation of websites available from often unknown sources means that scholars using the Internet need to exercise critical judgment as they "surf the Net." There is nothing magical about the Internet that makes information gleaned there automatically worthwhile. Treat online resources as you would any other sources. You will want to be especially cautious when relying on fact claims and assertions from untested, unknown, or unidentifiable sources—but then you'll want to be just as cautious about hardcopy sources of unknown pedigree, too. And, of course, you should always critically assess claims made by even the most prestigious of sources—whether hardcopy, digital, or online.

It is one thing to *use* the Internet as one source among others, and quite another to *exclusively rely on it* because it is easier to use search-engines to do research and then download whatever you find, than it is to dig through hardcopy sources. You'll deprive yourself if you ignore the Internet, and you'll deprive yourself if you ignore off-line, undigitized sources, as well. (By the way, I have included some interesting philosophy websites in the Bibliography of this book.)

One last word. It has always been tempting to confuse form with substance. We tend to give more credence to impressive looking books than to poorly produced ones. Some people assume that if something is published in a magazine or newspaper it must be reliable. This tendency to confuse *the method of delivery with what is delivered* carries over to websites and CD-ROMs. Impressive graphics, animation, hyper-links, and sound can greatly enhance the content of online and digital sources. But because the computer-assisted market is so huge, entrepreneurs are rushing forward with thousands of slick offerings. Keep in mind, amidst all the hype, that a CD-ROM encyclopedia, for example, is still an *encyclopedia*. If an encyclopedia is an appropriate source for a paper, then a good CD-ROM version offers the benefits of easy search features and fast copying. Do not confuse the mode of delivery with what is delivered.

THE DOG ATE MY COMPUTER

> **Self-justification is worse than the original offense.**
> *Sheik Ziaudin*

Don't confuse *explanations* with *excuses*. Although there are legitimate excuses for failing to meet assignment deadlines and paper due dates, they are surprisingly rare. Printer jams, traffic jams, bathroom jams, dead car batteries, alarm clocks that don't alarm, and such are all the regular stuff of life. As such, they are *generally foreseeable*. That means that you should anticipate them in budgeting time to prepare and deliver the final draft of your paper.

This advice is especially significant in the case of major assignments with substantial lead time. If, for instance, you have been given four weeks to write a paper, your professor may be underwhelmed upon learning that you were still working on it at three a.m. the morning it was due. Or that you arrived at the college computer center to begin typing it one day before it was due. After teaching for almost thirty years, I'm still a bit bemused by the number of students who leave for campus an hour or so before a major assignment is due, only to discover (horrors) that on that one day in history—that very day—old faithful won't start and "*all my friends had already left.*" You get the idea. (The same considerations apply to getting to that big exam or job interview on time and well prepared.)

Don't be afraid to request special consideration when you have genuinely extenuating circumstances that are beyond your control. But don't violate your own sense of self-respect by pleading special circumstances when the circumstances are not special.

PART THREE

Student Wisdom

Would a sick person be helped
Merely by reading a medical text?

Shantiveda

Y*ou already possess most of the skills and abilities necessary to succeed in college.* Have you noticed how much time sports fans put into reading about their interests? How much time and energy people put into tinkering on their cars or decorating their homes or playing basketball? How much money is spent on hobbies? How much sweat, work, energy, and sacrifice? Have you noticed how easy it is to remember the date and starting time of the big game or concert—even if it's weeks away?

These are the very same habits and abilities that make successful students successful. The difference between spending two hours a night reading sports magazines and two hours studying philosophy is due as much to lack of interest and motivation as it is to lack of ability.

Part Three is a summary of lots of good advice, what I think of as *student wisdom*. Some of it will be new to you, but much of it will not. Combining new advice with reminders of what you already know about school success can strengthen your commitment to your education, and inspire you when the going gets rough.

Chapter 6 is chock-full of excellent time-saving and motivational tidbits. Chapter 7 contains time-tested guidelines for having rich, rewarding relationships with your professors. Chapter 8 is a distillation of expert tips on taking tests. The Bibliography for Beginning Philosophers lists a variety of effective manuals and reference materials that can smooth your educational journey.

Remember, when you enroll in college you are *asking* to be guided, evaluated, and certified as competent according to other people's standards. That is why a college degree is characterized as part of your *formal* education. Standards, practices, and curriculum are formalized.

Part of the social value of a college degree is the expectation of consistency and conformity associated with it. This is arbitrary in much the same way that requiring you to drive on the right side of a two-way street is arbitrary. Certainly you could drive just as well, perhaps even more comfortably, on the left side of the street—if you were the only one on the street.

CHAPTER 6

Motivation and Strategy for Getting the Most Out of College

The most valuable result of all education is to make you do the thing you have to do, when it ought to be done, whether you like it or not.

Thomas Huxley

Write down all the reasons you have for going to college. List your *real* reasons, not your *public* ones. If you are going to college because you need a degree to get a certain kind of job, say so. If you're going to college to put off getting a "real job," say so. Don't feel pressured to pretend that you want to broaden yourself if you're really in college because you don't know what else to do at this stage of your life. List as many reasons as you have. Almost any reason for going to college can be a good reason, if you learn something important while you're there.

This is a surprisingly valuable exercise. There's no substitute for actually writing your reasons down. Just thinking or talking about them is not as insightful. Do this exercise before reading any further. Whether you use the form on the next page, or other paper, *keep your list.*

MY REASONS FOR GOING TO COLLEGE

Take a moment to review your list. If you're like most students, you'll have a variety of reasons for being in college, including a general desire to learn, a desire for the social prestige attached to being a college graduate, and the hope that a degree will lead to a financially comfortable and personally rewarding career.

Whatever your current circumstances, note that *you have decided that going to college is better than all of the alternatives.* When you get discouraged, remind yourself that you are where you have decided it's best to be at the moment.

Keep your list handy, and read it when you need a boost: before tests; during difficult projects; when you're feeling sorry for yourself because you need to study but want to party or have more time for your family; whenever you wonder "Why am I doing this?" Note that these are *your* reasons. Add to your list as you discover additional reasons for going to college.

Regularly reassess your goals. An academic or vocational degree requires a significant investment of time, effort, and money. Failure to identify your own clear reasons for going to college can result in wasting all three.

At the same time, part of the educational process is ongoing self-discovery that often results in new goals, so don't be discouraged if your plans change two or three times during your college career. *The crucial thing is to be as clear as you can about your real goals. No one else's opinions about going to college can give you the energy and commitment required for college success.*

Here's a bit of advice that may anger some of the people in your life: *It's all right if this is not the time for you be in college.* You're the only one who can get deep enough into your motives to know what's right for you now. If you are not ready to concentrate and sacrifice, or if you have too many complications in your personal life, you may be wise to wait before going on with your education. You do not want to use up limited financial aid while you're distracted or poorly motivated. And you don't want a weak transcript, since a weak transcript won't help you get a job, and can make it difficult (or impossible) to go on with your education in the future.

On the other hand (philosophers always have another hand to cloud the issue), be very sure that you have exhausted all your resources before deciding to quit college. If you're worried about money or working too much, talk to a good financial aid advisor.

You might be eligible for a scholarship you've never heard of, or a loan, or additional work study. Find out what opportunities your college offers for child care, if that's a concern. Make sure you don't just need more rest, or eyeglasses, or to take one fewer course per term. Don't let one instructor or course stop you. Check on evening classes at your own and other nearby colleges if the only instructor for a required course is offensive to you.

REALITY CHECK

> **A good student is someone who has learned how to learn from anyone.**   *Richard Watson*

• **Learning is your responsibility.** The great philosophical teacher Socrates insisted that the teacher's task is to draw knowledge out of the pupil—not to pour information into "an empty vessel." If you approach your formal education as an active participant, not only are you more likely to learn more, you are also less likely to lay all blame on your teachers, textbooks, and courses when you encounter difficulty.

• **You probably lack the time and ability to change your teachers—and you don't need to.** Although you can help most of your teachers be better teachers by being a committed, helpful, and attentive student, you probably cannot change any of them. If you think about it, you'll realize that you are least likely to change the very worst teachers. But that's okay because:

• **Your can learn virtually any subject from virtually any teacher.** The fact of the matter—which students and professors hate to acknowledge—is that good teaching is not necessary for college success. How do we know this? We know because virtually everyone of us has personally survived bad teaching. We know this because we also know of students who fail in the presence of excellent teaching. We know this because, in most of our classes, some students thrive regardless of the teacher. And at this point it really doesn't matter what constitutes good and bad teaching.

Different reactions to the same teacher are bedrock facts of formal education. (Note: I'm only talking about bad *teaching* here, not bad *teachers*: Sexual predators, bullies, racists, and such, present more complex, utterly unacceptable cases, best dealt with cautiously and with help. In such cases, you probably cannot learn and have a right to expect help from your college.)

• **Don't confuse bad *teaching* with bad *teachers*.** If your teacher degrades you or others, engages in sexual harassment or expresses bigotry or prejudice to a degree that inhibits learning, you will need to take appropriate action. You should consult with a trusted counselor or other knowledgeable individual in such a serious case. Your remedies will range from talking things over with the teacher to going to the department head or a higher level administrator in very serious situations. If the problem is a serious personality or teaching style clash, you may have to choose between evils: sticking it out and doing your best, or dropping the class and taking it later from a different instructor. When you just cannot get along with a teacher, take appropriate, *informed* action on your own behalf.

• **Not all courses are entertaining, and not all entertaining professors are good teachers.** It is unreasonable to expect your professors to entertain you. That is not their job. Besides, persuasive power, charm, and charisma are unrelated to the quality of the lesson or message they sell. Since you are in college to learn how to think well for yourself, you will need to evaluate what you're taught; and it's tempting to be less critical of likable characters. Besides, more fundamentally, life itself is not always "entertaining," although I do believe that it is almost always interesting to interested minds. In some languages, "to bore" is a reflexive verb. You would say, for instance, "I bore myself in chemistry class," rather than, "Chemistry is boring." Boredom is in the mind of the impatient, incurious, or self-absorbed beholder.

• **A college degree is a minimal qualification for many opportunities; it is not, however, a necessary or sufficient condition for financial or social success, nor for personal happiness.** We know this because the world is chock-full of unhappy college graduates *and* happy college graduates. We know this because the world is chock-full of unhappy people who have not gone to college *and* happy people who have not gone to college. And we know this on a much deeper level because we have all been disappointed after acquiring some longed-for goal—just as we have all been surprised by our own positive reactions to some dreaded event, interpersonal encounter, or tough circumstance.

While it is certainly true that what constitutes "a college education" is always somewhat arbitrary, always a "work in progress," always "under revision," it is also true that one of the social expectations of formal academic certifications is a *core of conformity*. A city planning commission has a right to expect that any new engineering graduates it hires possess a core of experiences, skills, and capacities common to "being an engineer." You have a right to expect that your environmental ethics professor has a degree in philosophy with an emphasis on environmental studies, not, say, a degree in sociology, chemistry or arithmetic.

If there is no common core of standards, then having a degree in engineering from an accredited college would mean no more or less than having no degree, or inventing one. Now we all know of mediocre and incompetent doctors, lawyers, engineers, certified diesel mechanics, accountants, retinal surgeons, computer SYSOPS, amanuenses, and nurse anesthetists. We've all wondered: "How on earth did she ever pass the bar?" "Who hired him?" "I thought you had to be pretty sharp to graduate from Stanvard University. Was I ever wrong."

So what does this prove? Only that colleges, bar exams, board certifiers—like life itself—are not perfect. It does not prove that all standards are trivially arbitrary or that we are all qualified to certify ourselves.

HOW TO SET AND ACHIEVE REALISTIC GOALS

• **Identify *your* strengths and weaknesses as objectively as possible.** You can do this informally or go to the college counseling center for career interest and skills testing.

- **Respect *your* interests.** If you've always hated school, don't choose a major that requires years of it. If you've never liked children, don't plan to become a teacher just because that job market is good.

- **Respect *your* talents.** Take advantage of your natural abilities. If you're a natural socializer and conversationalist who's always been able to make feel people comfortable, and who can relate to practically anybody, you may be happier as a teacher or social worker than working alone as a research chemist or forest ranger.
  Be creative as you explore your options. A natural socializer might become a happy, first-rate hotel manager or cruise ship entertainment director instead of a teacher or social worker. On the other hand, maybe you've always been good with details, even as a child. You like order and instinctively arrange things logically. Academic and career areas that are subject to creative disarray and require subjective interpretation may not be your best choice. Drama, literature, working with small children, may frustrate you, but accounting, office management, computer processing may not.

- **When you have no clear direction, experiment.** Take any classes that interest you for two or three terms. See if they show a pattern. If they do, fashion your newly identified interests into a workable major. If absolutely nothing interests you, consider taking a break from college.

- **Take advantage of your school's career center.** There are probably many career options that you are not aware of. Get some expert help in identifying them.

- **Base your immediate goals on your current life circumstances.** Realistically consider family obligations, job requirements, the demands of specific courses, transportation needs (and time), and so forth, as you plan your educational strategy.

- **Continually monitor your *progress* and your *satisfaction*.** Modify your goals accordingly.

•   **Superman and Superwoman are fictional characters. They don't exist in real life.** You may discover that your state of mind and performance significantly improve by taking one less class a term, or working five fewer hours a week. While a certain amount of tension can be good for you, too much can result in overload and inefficiency.

•   **Remember that you can always change your mind.**

TIME MANAGEMENT

By the end of the first week of the term you should have a general idea of how much time you'll need for each of your classes. Counselors usually suggest allowing *three hours of study for every one hour of class.* Plan a tentative study schedule, allowing time for daily assignments, major projects, and test preparation. You can modify this schedule as experience warrants. Be sure to include regular leisure activity, exercise, and rest. Try to allow "flex time" for unexpected emergencies, for improvised social activities, and for other unforeseeable needs. *Academic counselors report that failure to establish and stick to a regular study schedule is the most common characteristic shared by students with poor grades, or who ultimately drop out of college.*

Use the simple form on the next page to get an idea of the kind of commitment you will need to make to succeed in college.

ESTABLISH A TIME BUDGET

(YOU HAVE 168 HOURS TO SPEND EACH WEEK)

Total hours spent on campus per week
(time in class, at team practices and games,
student government, in the library, labs)   _____

3 hours X _____ units for out-of-class study   _____

Total hours worked per week   _____

_____ hours for sleep X 7 nights   _____

Total hours per week for necessities
(cooking, eating, shopping, bathing, laundry,
yardwork, etc.)   _____

Total hours per week for family duties
(driving children to various activities, helping
with homework, helping other relatives,
attending church, and so forth)   _____

Total hours per week for exercise   _____

Total commuting hours per week   _____

TOTAL OBLIGATED HOURS PER WEEK   _____

TOTAL HOURS IN A WEEK   _____**168**_____

MINUS TOTAL OBLIGATED HOURS   —   _____

EQUALS FREE TIME PER WEEK   _____

ACCEPTING WHAT YOU CANNOT CHANGE

The wise Hasidic Rabbi Zusya once said, "When I get to heaven, they will not ask me, Why were you not Moses?, they will ask me, Why were you not Zusya?"

It can be frustrating when other people get better grades than you do without studying as much as you do. But the harsh fact is that the only value someone else's grades and study habits can have for you is informational. If you can learn something from them that will improve your comprehension, skills, and performance, good. If not, your best bet is to ignore the seeming injustice of it all.

It can be annoying when the instructor gives multiple-choice tests, and you excel at essays (or vice versa). It's doubly disturbing when the test questions are trivial or "irrelevant." But once you discover the instructor's style of testing, your best bet is to accommodate yourself to it.

You may wish to respectfully offer reasonable alternatives, but you must ultimately deal with the less-than-perfect tests you are given. This kind of accommodation is not the same thing as selling-out. It is grounded in academic realty. As a rule, students don't get to write or individualize their tests and assignments. Act the role of the wise student. Don't get trapped in the role of resentful would-be-instructor.

CHANGING WHAT YOU CAN

Respectfully exert what influence you can to improve your courses, but learn when to cease in these efforts and get on with doing as well as you can, given the particular demands of the course.

•   **Don't punish yourself.** If a course is *truly* beyond your current abilities, or the instructor is demeaning, unprofessional, unprepared, and so forth, get out.

•   **Don't short-change yourself.** If you've been attending class and keeping up with assignments, trust your gut reactions. Go ahead, ask the questions that occur to you during lecture, make thoughtful comments. Give yourself credit for being able to identify issues that need clarification. Even if your instructor modifies or corrects what you say, you will have learned something, reinforced your self-respect, and polished your skills at rational discourse. How can you lose with that combination?

• **In any area where you are experiencing frustration and difficulty, consider a fresh approach.** If you've been studying philosophy after dinner, try studying at some other time. Try sitting in a different seat. Change the way you take notes. The point is, if things aren't working well, don't be too quick to dismiss alternatives. Something that seems silly or unpromising may surprise you. (Of course, if the new approach only makes things worse, stop using it.) I know this sounds obvious and too simple, but you'd be surprised at how many students refuse to try new approaches because they prejudge them as unhelpful.

• **Distinguish between accommodating yourself to the unavoidable inequities of academic life and serious unethical inequalities. Not all compromises involve your very essence.**

AVOIDING FALSE COMPARISONS: THE TRAGIC LESSON OF JOHN HENRY

> As long as you have to defend the imaginary self that you think is important, you will lose your peace of heart. As soon as you compare that shadow with the shadows of other people, you lose all joy, because you have begun to trade in unrealities, and there is no joy in things that do not exist.
>
> *Thomas Merton*

You may know the folk legend of John Henry. John Henry worked on the railroad, using two nine-pound hammers to drive the steel spikes that hold the rails to the ties. Shortly after the invention of the steam-engine, the railroad companies began to replace steel drivers with steam-powered machines that would ultimately put thousands of men out of work. According to the legend, John Henry challenged one of the new machines to a spike-driving contest, and "won." Swinging a hammer in each hand, the powerful John Henry drove more spikes than the machine. He was so exhausted from the effort that he "laid down his hammer and he died."

Many people see the story of John Henry in terms of one man's courage in the fight against the replacement of human beings by machines. There's another lesson, too. We can kill ourselves trying to be what we're not. John Henry was not a machine. He could not be expected to do a machine's work. No amount of desire, courage, or righteousness could change the harsh reality of John Henry's relation to the new machine.

You may have untapped potential and room to grow, but you are a particular individual and no other. You cannot become the student sitting next to you, your mother, pal, teacher, or fictionalized ideal. Learn from others, but don't condemn yourself for not being them. Don't exhaust yourself trying to be someone you're not.

If you're interested in this issue of "becoming yourself," you can read more about it in Chapter 5 The Naturalist: Aristotle, in *Archetypes of Wisdom,* Third Edition. The following passage from the Trappist monk and philosopher **Thomas Merton (1915-1968)** is from that chapter. Reread it when you're doing a job on yourself for not being someone else:

> Many [people] . . . never become the [person] who is called for by all the circumstances of their individual lives. They waste their years in vain efforts to be some other [person]. . . . For many absurd reasons, they are convinced that they are obliged to become somebody else. . . . They wear out their minds and bodies in a hopeless endeavor to have somebody else's experiences or write somebody else's poems or express sómebody else's spirituality.

• **Sometimes it takes courage to keep on doing something, and sometimes it takes courage to quit (especially if others will be disappointed).** If John Henry had paid closer attention to himself, he would have known that he was taxing his heart beyond its endurance. Even though he "won" the challenge, he lost in the long run. It's sometimes better to quit early than quit later. (Of course, this principle has a corollary that works in the other direction. You shouldn't expect others to "carry you," or meet responsibilities that you are capable of meeting. So be sure that you're quitting for good reasons, and not just to avoid studying hard, and so forth.)

• **Resist comparisons that lead to resentment.** We all know that life is not particularly fair. Resentment won't improve your grades, and it can pollute your emotions in a way that actually interferes with good study habits.

• **March to your own beat.** If other people pressure you to proceed at a pace that's inappropriate for you, if they make fun of you for lacking certain skills, remind yourself that they will not suffer if you have to drop out of college, and they won't pay your student loans if you can't keep up. In other words, *you are the one who will pay the price if you fail to meet their expectations.* Your friends and family shouldn't expect you to make their credit card payments—and they shouldn't expect you to make their "life payments." If they do expect you to, resist in the best way you can.

• **Nurture a commitment to excellence; determine always to seek your own highest level, given an honest assessment of your actual circumstances.** Your goal here is not to impress others. It is not even to impress yourself. Your goal is not to inflate or diminish yourself, but to nourish your finer attributes. Recall some occasion on which you "surpassed yourself," refused to succumb to tempting distractions or the "easier, softer way," and persisted when part of you cried out to quit or settle for the minimal standard. Perhaps you stuck it out through the grueling weeks of August football drills, stuck it out when you felt like collapsing. Perhaps you signed up for tutoring help in a difficult algebra course, rather than dropping out. Perhaps you retyped an English essay when you realized that you could do better. And perhaps after all that effort, you didn't make the team, or got a D in Algebra or English. You got something else, though: a reinforced commitment to yourself, a commitment to high aspirations and quality effort. Far better to fail now and then at worthy goals, goals that enhance your spirit, than to succeed at the trite, true, and safe. (Dangerous advice, perhaps. But, then, philosophy has always been dangerous.)

WHAT IT *REALLY* COSTS TO GO TO COLLEGE

> Do not forget that going to college is your choice. Resist thinking that you "have" to do your assignments. The reality is that you are being given the *privilege* of doing your assignments. No fixed law of nature, morality, or society forces you to go to college or take a philosophy course. Going to college and taking philosophy courses are the clearly marked price tags for something of greater value: a good education and presumably greater opportunities for a good life.

• **Remind yourself that the full price of your education includes more than the monetary cost of fees and supplies.** You must pay with time, effort, and a temporarily modified social life. You will get the best education by paying full price. Trying to "have it all" commonly results in frustration, anxiety, fatigue, and increased risk of failure.

• **Regularly tell yourself that being a college student is only a temporary condition.** College may seem to go on forever, but it doesn't. You will have a "real life" someday. (And if you're like many of us, you'll look back on your years in college as "the good old days.")

• **The typical 3 unit semester course meets for less than 48 hours.** That's right: *less than two full days of class time*. If you study three hours for every class-hour, you'll add only six days, bringing the total to a week and one day. Generously allowing another two full weeks for total time spent on term papers and so forth, one three-unit class involves a total of three weeks and one day. And for those students who do not study three hours for every hour spent in class, a three-unit class takes even less time.

   If you take four courses, that's only eight days in class per semester, or 16 days per year (20 days per year if you take five courses). If you graduate from a two-year program, you may be in class for *35-40 days*. You can double that for the typical bachelor's degree to *70-80 days*. (Typically, students who take five or six years to get their bachelor's degrees spend additional hours at work, not in class, so the total stays the same.) Even adding the hours needed for studying, and the cost of tuition, and supplies, and room and board, college is a bargain.

• **Think of going to college as your primary job.** Job requirements include: regular attendance; doing assignments; spending money on supplies instead of pizza and beer; listening to ideas you don't like or have no personal interest in; taking good notes; paying attention; and studying, studying, studying.

CHEERFULLY PAYING THE PRICE: EPICTETUS'S OBULUS

• **When you get frustrated and resent paying the price, review this lesson from the _Enchiridion_ of the Stoic sage Epictetus (c. 50-130):**

> You will be unjust then and insatiable, if you do not part with the price, in return for which . . . things are sold, and if you wish to obtain them for nothing. Well, what is the price of lettuces? An obulus perhaps. If then a man gives up the obulus and receives the lettuces, and if you do not give up the obulus and do not receive the lettuces, do not suppose that you receive less than he who has got the lettuces; for as he has the lettuces, so you have the obulus which you did not give . . .

If another student "gives up the obulus" by devoting time to philosophy, and by studying harder and more frequently than you do, don't compound your problems by resenting her better grade. She has a good grade in philosophy; you have your obulus (time used for other things).

Perhaps you're thinking, "But it is not that simple. I have a job and family—the other student doesn't. It's easy for her to study. I'd like to see what kind of grades she gets in my circumstances." Put that curiosity to rest, and review the earlier section on false comparisons. Remind yourself that you will never be able to see what kind of grades another student would get in your circumstances because *you* are an essential component of what makes your circumstances *your* circumstances. (And, of course, you *really don't know* how hard or easy it is for others to study.)

And whether or not life is "fair" is a deep philosophical problem that you have a lifetime to wrestle with. Right now, you need to maximize your actual circumstances. Think carefully about the "obuluses" in your life. Are you perhaps trying to "clip the coin a trifle" and not pay the full price? If so, you need to decide if the quality of your education (and all that is connected with it) warrants more effort and sacrifice while you're in college. If you are truly out of resources, and cannot pay the price, then you need to deal with that.

It's probably not fair that some people have it easier than others. But if life is not fair, then there's no reason to waste time harping on it, or foolishly waiting for someone or something to make it fair. Maybe they shouldn't charge a whole obulus for a lettuce, but until you are in a position to open a market or grow your own lettuce, about all you can do is decide to keep the obulus *or* acquire the lettuce.

As long as you're paying for a college education—and every student pays something—you might as well pay what it costs to get a good one. (And you might as well get your obulus's worth by studying and learning. Otherwise, you'll be like a man who pays an obulus for a head of lettuce and then only nibbles on a few leaves and then lets it rot. What a waste—of an obulus and a head of lettuce.)

A COLLEGE EDUCATION *IS* WORTH THE EFFORT

• **Lack of a college degree is a burden in today's economy, no matter what else affects your chances for a satisfying job.** Most students go to college in the hopes that having a college degree will lead to a high paying, satisfying job. Unfortunately, things aren't that simple. As more and more people graduate from college, the marketplace significance of having a college education diminishes. Ironically, that means that *the significance of **not** having a college education **increases**.* As a college degree becomes the minimum, its lack becomes a serious impediment to future job seekers.

And, clearly, as more people earn college degrees, the quality of your transcript matters more and more.

• **Think of your transcript as a kind of "credit report."** It takes ten years to overcome the negative effects of a bankruptcy on a person's credit history. It can also take many years to overcome a weak college transcript. What makes a transcript "weak?" Obviously, a low grade point average is a detriment on a transcript. So are lots of withdrawals and lots of fluff courses. When employers and graduate school admissions officers look at a big pile of transcripts and applications, they need criteria for awarding their limited jobs or scholarships. Consequently, just about everything in your application packet is important: letters of recommendation, work history, hobbies—and the courses you took and the grades you received.

• **All the effort and careful attention will pay off.** To begin with the philosophical point first, regardless of the kind of job you get, your college education should provide you with reasoning skills, interests, cultural baggage, and character traits that will help you cope with life. On the socio-economic front, Lunenfeld and Lunenfeld report in *College Basics*, that Anthony Patrick Carnevale, Ph. D., of the American Society for Training and Development, compared the potential lifetime earnings of two students, one without and one with a college degree. Dr. Carnevale calculated that the college degree would be worth about $631,000 in additional income.

• **What about all those Ph.D.'s driving cabs and flipping burgers?** Keep in mind that the jobs requiring a doctorate are relatively rare. Many people pursue a Ph. D. hoping to get one of the few jobs in their narrow specialty. Associate of Arts, vocational degrees, and Bachelor of Arts degrees are in far greater demand. But more importantly—and realistically—*a college degree provides a greater range of job opportunities, not a guaranteed job.* Landing a good job also depends on luck and such personal characteristics as a willingness to be flexible early in your job search, choice of major, and willingness to live where the good jobs in your field are. Lastly, some very satisfied people (with and without Ph. D.'s) drive cabs and flip burgers. **Socrates (c. 470-399 B. C.)** was a brick mason, **Lao-tzu (c. 575 B. C.)** was a low level bureaucrat, and **Baruch Spinoza (1632-1677)** was a lens grinder—three examples of wise people who deliberately *chose* very ordinary jobs.

> Good habits are good habits—in college and in "real life." Going to college helps us develop and refine our coping skills. To survive and thrive during a typical college education you must learn to concentrate on what others are saying. You will learn to learn from people whether or not you like them or find them attractive or interesting. You will learn to "perform" in the face of criticism. You will be encouraged to get to "work" on time, and you will learn how to deal with different kinds of "bosses" (teachers) and "co-workers" (other students). You will learn computer skills, researching skills, critical thinking skills. And if you do not resist, you will learn to enjoy learning and to value hard work in the pursuit of excellence.
>
> All in all, quite a bargain.

A NOTE OF ENCOURAGEMENT
FOR PART-TIME STUDENTS

According to the American Council on Education, there are more part-time students than ever before. Today, more than 40% of all college students are part-timers, and analysts expect the proportion of part-time students to increase into the foreseeable future. At many colleges, part-time students outnumber full-time students many times over. If you are one of these students, do your very best to make college a priority. Here are some ways to do that:

• **Write out a schedule at the start of every new school term.** Remember that failure to stick to a schedule is perhaps the greatest cause of frustration and failure for college students. (See page 105.)

• **Regularly focus your attention on the importance and value of your long-term goals.** Consult your list of reasons for going to college. Add to it. Remind yourself *why* you are juggling family life, a job, social activities, and college: You want a satisfying life for yourself and any family you may have, and you have realistically determined that a college education is necessary for that life.

•   **Read and listen to inspiring stories about struggling to get ahead.** Think of relatives who have worked hard to support you. Think of people you admire who worked hard and struggled for a mighty goal.

•   **Put your frustrations in perspective.** You may be very, very, very busy, and very, very, very, poor, and very, very, very stressed out at times, *but* people have and are suffering as much or more than you, and surviving, and even growing. This suggestion is not meant to trivialize your hardships, but to help you endure and master them. *If life has dealt you a more difficult hand than others, you have all the more reason to persist with your studies and give yourself every opportunity to have a better future than you will probably have if you drop out of college.*

•   **Take advantage of every support system you can find.** Many colleges provide day care for students' children. See if you qualify. Most colleges have tutorial centers, reading and writing labs, access to computers, health clinics, and special, overlooked scholarships for all sorts of things: unmarried mothers, textbook money, first-generation students, members of different ethnic groups, and so on. Ask around and shop around until you find a good advisor or counselor.

•   **A six-year degree is still a degree—and a degree is what you're after.** If it takes you longer to graduate than it takes full-time students, so be it. No matter how angry or frustrated this may make you, don't let it stop you. The Stoic writer **Seneca (c. 4 BC-65 AD)** said, "The greater the torment, the greater shall the glory be." If you persist, you will not only have a college degree or certificate, but you will have become a stronger, wiser, more appreciative human being in the process. That's quite a payoff.

> **All things excellent are as difficult as they are rare.**
> *Baruch Spinoza*

SELF-HELP REVIEW

• **Activate to motivate.** The philosophical amanuensis, Margaret L. Malone, uses this formula as reminder that—paradoxically and frustratingly—we must often "act as if" before we "feel like it." That is, *spontaneously inspired motivation does not always arrive in time.* Consequently, we are better served to take helpful, responsible, reasonable action when we need to, rather than wait until we want to. Fortunately, action is itself a tonic, and almost always reduces, if it does not completely abolish, lack of energy, lack of commitment, lack of motivation.

• **HALT!** That's not an order, it's an acronym, an easily remembered abbreviation for the formula: "Don't let yourself get too **H**ungry, too **A**ngry, too **L**onely, or too **T**ired." The Classical Greeks and Romans believed in "a sound mind in a sound body," and contemporary science suggests that they were right. We learn best when our basic physical, emotional, and mental needs are all met.

• **Take the "walking cure."** The poet David Grayson said "There is a poem in stretched legs," and today we know that even relatively mild exercise reduces anxiety and increases our sense of well-being and happiness. Some psychologists even treat mild depression with exercise and attribute some anxieties to "an overactive mind in an underactive body."

• **When in doubt, talk it out.** Sometimes the simple act of discussing problems generates solutions. Even if it doesn't, it almost always provides mental and emotional relief, and restores balance and perspective.

• **Meet your obligations to yourself as well as to your family, friends, and employer in a balanced way.** You are entitled to a good education, and do not need to feel guilty for taking time for yourself to get one. You also have other responsibilities. If you fail to meet them adequately, you may find yourself distracted by guilt. If you fail to give yourself enough time to learn, you may find yourself drained by anger and resentment. Balance can be difficult to find, but it pays off.

• **Be flexible in all but the essentials.** Stick to your guns on important matters, but cut yourself slack on all others.

• **Study when you can and *regularly*, not just before major tests.** Not only will this improve your grades, skills, and comprehension, it will reinforce the message that learning is an integral part of your life, not something you do only under pressure. It also reduces unhealthy anxiety—a real killer.

• **Make a supreme effort to have read every assignment at least once *before* class.** You may not be able to study every page of all of your assignments before every class, but you can quickly read ahead of your professors for every class. Naturally, the more time you can devote to preclass reading, the better, but even a quick reading of assigned material will pay off. You will be familiar with the purpose of each lecture or discussion. You will be more comfortable asking questions if you are familiar with the material (and hence more willing to ask questions). You will feel less anxious when you are prepared, and will remember and understand better than if you were tense or uninformed.

• **Study on schedule.** Do not wait to study until weekends and immediately before tests and assignments are due. Even if your grades don't suffer when you fall into the clutches of procrastination and last-minute-itis, you will have robbed yourself of processing information for long-term retention and mastery. You will add anxiety to your already busy life. You will deprive yourself of full participation in class, since you won't be familiar with the material as it is covered. (Reminder: Academic counselors report that failure to establish and stick to a regular study schedule is the most common characteristic shared by students with poor grades, or who ultimately drop out of college.)

• **Get everything you are paying for.** Have you ever been glad to discover that a class has been canceled or let out early? Sure, a change of pace is great once in a while. It can be invigorating. You cannot help it when classes are canceled, but you can resist the defeatist attitude of "Ugh! I have to go to class." Do not drag yourself to class. Attend eagerly, grateful for the opportunity to learn something new in a pleasant environment. *College is the only*

*commodity I know of where people are happy when they don't get
everything they're paying for.*

- **Contribute to your course by being pleasant and well prepared.**
Students are sometimes surprised when they discover how much
their own attitudes affect their teachers. Just as it can be very difficult to learn from unprepared, hostile, low-energy, or bored
teachers, it can be very difficult to teach a class when just a few
students exhibit some of these traits. On the other hand, the presence of one or two eager, well-prepared, and courteous students always enhances the quality of a course. Imagine what the classroom
atmosphere would be like if everyone came to class eager and
well-prepared.

- **Take classes from the best instructors you can.** Don't take
classes just because they're easy. That's a form of stealing your own
time. Avoiding challenges diminishes your abilities and impedes
self-respect. (The best way to find good instructors is to ask around.
Ask everybody you meet to recommend instructors. You'll quickly
recognize the names of the best.)

- **Take at least one class you're afraid of—and stick it out.**
Simply completing a challenging class will boost your sense of self-
respect. It will show you that you have drive and discipline. And
you might discover new interests and abilities. Remember, *you* can
do difficult things!

- **Take at least one class for the sheer joy of it.** Break free of the
trap of the drudge, the student whose whole education is serious
and calculating, allowing no room for failures (often defined as
anything less than an A). A shriveled life is a pretty high price to
pay for a 4.0 GPA. If you view college as something to "get over
with," you will rob yourself of the *personal enrichment* that
should be part of any real education. There is nothing wrong with
the practical, job-preparation part of contemporary higher education. But so much more is possible, if you want it.

- **Drop classes only when absolutely necessary.** A high GPA
ᵒompanied by a high percentage of dropped courses is a red flag

to employers as well as to admission committees of professional schools. Do well the first time.

• **Feel free to pick your own major: Remember, it's your life.** The late mythologist Joseph Campbell used to say, "There's no greater tragedy than to get to the top of the ladder and realize you're on the wrong wall."

• **When you feel like you'll never get done, think of this Buddhist proverb: "The journey is the destination."** There is no rule against enjoying philosophy and college. Besides, you certainly do not want to be the kind of person who would say. "Well that's it for me. I've learned enough. My education is complete."

> **However much you study, you cannot know without action.**
> *Saadi of Shiraz*

THE BIGGEST AVOIDABLE MISTAKES
COLLEGE STUDENTS MAKE

Here's a helpful list of avoidable mistakes college students make.

• **Not making college a priority.** This can be difficult if you are a part-time student, or have family obligations, or work long hours at a job—but not making college a priority is one of the worst things you can do to your chances for a good education.

• **Poor course selection.** Consult experienced students, and select courses by professors, not just course names.

• **Signing up for too many or too few classes.** Freshmen should be especially careful not to overload their schedules the first term. At the same time, taking too few classes can lead to dropping out of college if progress toward a degree takes too long. Ironically, taking too few classes can be worse than having a full schedule, if your light load gives you a false sense of security that makes sticking to a study schedule difficult. Also, taking too few credit courses can result in loss of financial aid.

• **Poor study habits.** Poor study habits include not studying enough, studying when distracted or tired, studying in bed, studying under the influence of drugs.

• **Making false economies.** Given the money-focused nature of this culture, it's not surprising that college students try to save as much money as possible. But sometimes, saving money gets to be pretty expensive. One of the worst tradeoffs you can make is trying to get by without purchasing your own copies of all course materials: textbooks, workbooks, recommended readings. Studying is hard enough, without the added complication of trying to budget additional travel time to get to the library to use reserve copies of the text—only to find that they're unavailable. Book-sharing partners change their minds or schedules. False economies are particularly destructive when they're the result of indulgences such as spending limited resources for fancy wheels for your truck or expensive hairdos, and the like, instead of investing those resources in a good education, when it is offered. No one is suggesting that you live like a monk (but in some cases, a simpler, more dedicated lifestyle might be a wise idea for a while.)

• **Social extremism.** You may be tempted to drop out of college if you delete all social involvement and fun from your life. You may be tempted to drop out of college if you are too busy socializing and having "the college experience." Don't lose sight of the fact that getting a good education is the most important part of that experience, and being well educated includes learning how to find a balance between workaholism and dissolute self-indulgence.

• **Freshman ego.** The "freshman ego" is an inflated sense of superiority that some college students retain long after they stop being freshman. This mind-set occurs when the natural joy and delight of being new to higher education, of having optimistic, idealistic goals, and of sometimes seeing through hypocrisy and pernicious compromise, are misinterpreted as signs of profound insight and wisdom. The freshman ego is ready to fix the world. Often, the freshman ego's concerns are real and important: the environment, social justice, poverty, and so forth. But dogmatism (unquestioning faith in the correctness and superiority of our own ideas) is not just a hindrance to learning; it often alienates others, making it more difficult to communicate our ideas to them.

BE COOL ABOUT BEING COOL ABOUT SCHOOL

A word of caution. What follows is being written by a middle-aged philosophy professor who is never quite sure what the current "cool" term is. Over the course of my educational career (which began when I was six years old and continues to the present), the cool terms have included: Hip, hep, beat, groovy, way out, boss, bitchin', bad, rad, radical, neat, fine, excellent, beautiful, copacetic, smooth, mellow, phat—and cool. But there is a deadly kind of "cool" attitude that reflects aloofness, disdain, and detachment that has always been around, and it can really interfere with your enjoyment and success in school. That's the kind of cool this section is about.

• **Sometimes, being cool can work against succeeding in college.** Being "cool" sometimes manifests itself as adopting a style that is deliberately unresponsive, aloof, anti-establishment, and distant—detached and "in control" of every gesture, word, and emotion. That kind of cool sits in the back of the classroom. Cool slouches and smirks. Cool sleeps in class. Cool wears shades. Unresponsive cool doesn't take notes. Aloof cool doesn't lug around a backpack full of textbooks. Distant cool cuts class. Antisocial cool shows up hungover or loaded, whispers and passes notes in class— makes its disdain very clear. Such attitudes can easily lead to a profound sense of detachment from class. They interfere with listening and learning. This kind of "cool" may attract unfavorable attention from professors, and from more serious, "uncool," students, which will simply reinforce an "us-against-them" sense of detachment.

• **Aloof cool's tendency to "dis" character traits that lead to academic and socio-economic success is a serious stumbling block to learning.** By "disrespecting," that is by mocking and ridiculing, students who worry about their grades and who fully participate in class, aloof cool increases the risk of shutting us off from succeeding at anything besides being cool.

Although there are no guaranteed paths to personal, social, and economic well-being, we have already seen that many of the same traits that make a successful, satisfied student pay off beyond college. On the other hand, strong sense of contempt for others is not conducive to good work or school relationships. Effort devoted to "beating the system" (through cheating on tests, scamming financial aid, purchasing term papers, conning professors) robs the cool of the sorts of experiences that foster lasting self-respect. *For the cool, "beating the system" reinforces a false sense of superiority.* This feeling of superiority is false because it does not take great ability to cheat teachers with large classloads, or who have more significant tasks than catching every attempt to get away with something. Further, there's always the risk that by adopting the view that education is just one more cynical game, the distantly cool student creates a mind-set that projects shabby cynicism to other aspects of life.

• **Cool's range of influence is surprisingly limited.** Cool is most appealing to people who have a heightened need for validation from other people. Cool is not very influential in graduate school, at most jobs, when applying for a loan, in court, and so on. It's one thing to be selectively cool, but being defensively or aggressively cool can be self-limiting if it becomes a major goal in your life.

• **Affirmative cool is wise cool.** Affirmative, or "hot," passionate cool is an attitude of delight, respect, and attraction. This is cool as a term of high praise. College is cool in this way. Studying is cool in this way of being cool. Participating in class, showing enthusiasm, being involved are wise cool. If you like being cool, be cool enough to maximize your time in college. Even if the sheer joys of learning and mastery don't move you, the opportunity to live a richer life, a life of more choices and opportunities, can be a sufficient motive to be a good student. And that's really cool.

> To know what you do not know is best.
> To pretend to know what you do not know is a disease.
> *Laotse*

CHAPTER 7

Relating to Your Professor

Remember, you are working for yourself. You have doubtless heard, "I have a theme to write for __ . I have thirty pages to read for __ . I have ten pages to write for old __ . " Nothing could be further from the truth. You do a lot of work in school, but none of it is done for the teacher. You are working to develop not the teacher but yourself.

William H. Armstrong

Your professor wants you to succeed in acquiring new knowledge, learning and polishing new skills, discovering new facets of yourself, and by experiencing first-hand the many pleasures of the mind. Just as it is to your advantage to have a competent, friendly, courteous, professional instructor, it is to your instructor's advantage to have eager, inquisitive, hard working, and courteous students. It's helpful to keep that in mind when you interact with your professor.

The following is a collection of tips and guidelines for making the most of your interactions with your professor.

• **Always respect your teacher's role and position, regardless of your feelings about the person.** If you have the unfortunate experience of being stuck with a teacher you find difficult or ineffective, remind yourself that in spite of his or her weaknesses, this teacher has probably completed several years of higher education. At the very least, he or she is entitled to the respect due the *position of teacher.*

• **Communicate, communicate, communicate.** Your professor cannot read your mind. It is *your responsibility* to let him or her know when something is not clear, or whenever you have a special concern. Since you are responsible for all assignments, it is important to understand exactly what is expected.

• **Study the course syllabus as soon as you receive it.** Learn what is important to your instructor. Learn the location of his or her office, the designated office hours and office phone number.

• **Address your instructor the way he or she prefers.** Some instructors prefer to be addressed as Mr., Mrs., or Ms., others as Doctor or Professor. Simple courtesy and pragmatism suggest that you do as requested. *Although some instructors prefer to be addressed by their first names, do not use an instructor's first name until invited to do so.*

• **Request, don't demand.** The Taoists teach (correctly, I think) that "Forceful actions rebound." That means that aggression breeds aggression, attack breeds counterattack. No matter how nervous, frightened, or angry you are, try not to approach your instructor in a rude, belligerent, demanding, or sarcastic manner. Doing so may pollute the interaction before it begins. Instructors can be just as insecure as you are. When attacked, some of them immediately become defensive and resistant to your message.

• **Speak for yourself.** Unless seriously injured or incarcerated, do not ask parents, friends, coaches, or other instructors to speak for you to your instructor.

• **Stay in touch.** If you have to miss a few classes or cannot meet an assignment deadline or make a test date, contact your instructor as soon as you know you will not be there. Do not rely on others to convey your message. Do not just assume that you will or won't be allowed an extension. It's your responsibility to meet all requirements, or make your own arrangements for not doing so.

• **Think about *how* you say things.** Most instructors do not appreciate remarks such as: "I missed class Tuesday. Did we do anything important?" or "That's dumb. Why'd we waste class time on it?"

Consider these more effective alternatives: "I'm sorry I was not in class Tuesday. What can I study to help make up for what I missed?" "I'm not clear as to the significance of this material? Could you explain it further for me?" If you hate philosophy, there's no particular reason to volunteer that fact to the person who's devoted a lifetime to it.

• **Don't flirt with or date your instructor. Period.** Even if you think your involvement has no bearing on your grades, other students won't believe that. They'll feel cheated. And they *will* find out about your involvement. If you break up, you may find yourself in the awkward position of being graded by your "ex."

• **Don't tolerate sexual harassment.** If your instructor flirts with you, makes inappropriate personal comments, or somehow makes you uncomfortable in a sexual way, you are in a delicate spot. Tell your instructor you are not comfortable. If that does not take care of the problem, talk to the instructor's immediate supervisor.

• **Let your instructor know what works and what doesn't.** Instructors get less useful feedback about their courses than you might guess. Vague compliments or criticisms ("Great class!" or "Boy, was that boring!") don't help us develop and retain good features and modify, or delete, bad ones. Be specific when commenting on what works or doesn't work.

• **Share your enthusiasm.** Perhaps nothing delights a teacher more than expressions of interest in a course. Ask for additional works by a favorite philosopher. Stop by and tell your instructor about a connection you've made between something from philosophy class and another class, or that has some special relevance to your daily life.

• **Avoid appeals to pity.** If you have a special request, make it in as straightforward a way as possible. Avoid committing the logical fallacy known as **appeal to pity**. *An appeal to pity occurs when a person attempts to advance a conclusion by evoking feelings of pity in others, when pity is irrelevant to the conclusion at hand.* If you have special circumstances that interfere with getting an assignment in on time or taking a test, you should certainly inform your instructor in a timely way. If you anticipate a persistent pattern of such requests, you may need to take the course at some other time. Appealing to pity is unwise because you never know if it will move your professor to help you, or be perceived as excuse-making, avoidance, or manipulation. (Your fundamental obligation of self-respect is incompatible with making fallacious appeals to pity.)

> Remember, when you just cannot get along with your teacher, take appropriate, *informed* action on your own behalf. If your teacher degrades you or others, engages in sexual harassment or expresses bigotry or prejudice to a degree that inhibits learning, you will need to take appropriate action. You should consult with a trusted counselor or other knowledgeable individual in such a serious case. Your remedies will range from talking things over with the teacher to going to the department head or a higher level administrator in very serious situations. If the problem is a personality or teaching style clash, you may have to choose between evils: sticking it out and doing your best, or dropping the class and taking it later from a different instructor.

CONFERENCES WITH YOUR PROFESSOR

• **Always introduce yourself.** Until you're sure that your instructor knows your name, always introduce yourself and identify the particular course section you attend.

• **Make a good faith effort to meet during scheduled office hours.** You don't want to waste your instructor's time, or give the impression that you are irresponsible. So don't be irresponsible.

• **Keep your appointments, or notify the instructor or the department secretary if you cannot.** This simple courtesy is also pragmatic: It keeps you on good terms with your professor. Keep track of appointments, and if you miss one, notify your instructor as soon as possible. Whatever your reason for missing the appointment—even if it's just forgetting—don't simply avoid mentioning it. If you don't have a good excuse, simply apologize; if you have an excuse,

use it. The worst thing to do when you have any kind of problem with a class is nothing. Your philosophy instructor wants to help you succeed. He or she will work with you if you make a solid effort—and if you communicate.

- **Be on time.** Politely, let your professor know you have arrived.

- **Knock before opening a closed office door.** If your professor's office door is closed, don't just open it.

- *After carefully studying*, **if there is still something you don't understand or have a problem with, write it out clearly and specifically before going to your professor.** Often, the very act of formulating a clear question or statement regarding a problem will make the answer clear to you—or point you to the answer. When this does not work, your statement will still be a great help to your professor, making it easier for him or her to help you.

- **If you have a number of questions, bring a written list of the main points you wish to discuss.** It's easy to forget even the most important things during a discussion. If you have a written list, you can make sure that you've covered everything that's important to you.

- **If you're discussing a grade, bring the graded test or paper with you.** Don't expect your instructor to remember the details of every test or paper.

- **Cool off before you discuss something that's really bothering you.** Don't rush right over and complain about a test or paper grade based on your first reaction. Wait at least one day. Carefully reassess the issue. If it continues to be important to you, consult your instructor.

LETTERS OF RECOMMENDATION
(AND BEYOND)

As I learned during my sophomore year in college (see Preface), it is difficult for most instructors to write a persuasive letter of recommendation based only on a student's grades. The most effective letters of recommendation refer to your unique qualities. Get to know three or four instructors well enough for them to recommend you personally.

As the term implies, a *letter of recommendation* is a written evaluation attesting to your abilities, and recommending that you be viewed favorably as a candidate for scholarships, financial aid, admissions to academic and vocational programs, or a job. Letters of recommendation may be sent directly to those requesting them, or they may be held by your college's placement office, in a file known as a *dossier*. Your dossier will also contain your current transcript. Check to see if your school offers this service. The great advantage of having a dossier on file is that you don't need to ask for letters over and over, and you don't have to worry about losing track of them. Also, your instructor may no longer be at the college if you request a letter some time after you've completed the course. But if you've established a dossier, whenever you need to, you just place an order to have your dossier sent to whomever receives your job or school application, and the placement office mails out an official copy, for a modest handling fee. You can usually add to your dossier, as you get more letters of recommendation.

Because they free their writers to be very candid, the most effective letters of recommendation are not seen by their subjects. Don't be disturbed if you don't get to see your letters. If you are afraid of getting a negative evaluation from a professor, do not ask him or her for a letter. If you are given the choice between a letter you will be allowed to read or a "blind" letter, the blind letter may be a better bet because it will be interpreted as being more honest than a letter written with the knowledge that you will read it.

The most effective letters of recommendation are written by individuals with the training and experience to recognize superior merit or promise. They are personalized, and are based on sufficient relevant contact with you and your work. Keep this in mind when choosing people to write your letters of recommendation.

The time to deal with letters of recommendation is *immediately*. Even if you aren't sure you'll need any, play it safe and assume that you will. It can be difficult to write effective recommendations for students years after they've taken a course. With that in mind, here's a strategy for getting good letters of recommendation. This strategy pays off in other ways, too.

- **No matter what your present goals are, proceed with the assumption that at some point in your life you will need letters of recommendation from at least three of your professors.**

- **Drop by and just say hello.** Stop by and introduce yourself to your professors early in the term. You don't have to make a production of it or engage in "kissing up." Explain why you're taking the class, what you hope to gain from it, what your educational plans are, and so forth.

- **Speak up in class.** Show interest in your courses by being an active participant. Make thoughtful comments—*if you are current with your studies.*

- **Stop by when things are going *well*.** Reintroduce yourself, discuss what you've learned, what progress you've made, and so forth.

- **Perform at a level worthy of an honest recommendation.** Colleges, professional programs, and potential employers look at more than just grades. Your "performance" includes: responsibility (Did you meet deadlines? Did you attend class regularly?); reliability (Did you follow instructions? Did you pay attention to details? Did you proofread your papers?); teachability (Did you give new ideas a fair hearing?); maturity (Did you take criticism well and refrain from blaming others for your problems?); citizenship (Were you respectful of others? Did you do your part to make it a good class?); self-motivation (Did you sustain a high level of effort without having to be pushed constantly?); creativity (Did you think for yourself and add your own personal style to your coursework?).

• **Don't be afraid to request a recommendation just because you didn't get an A or B in a course.** Assess your *overall performance* in light of all relevant factors, not just grades. Although grades tend to be the chief markers of value in academia, other factors count, too. Character matters in college, as in the rest of life. My personal sense of things is that certain personal traits, beginning with a good work ethic, a realistic sense of self, modesty, integrity, and civility, matter more to long-term well-being than high grades and intellectual cleverness. I am usually pleased to recommend students who show these qualities in my classes, regardless of their grades.

There are many kinds of recommendation: purely academic, vocational, personal character, growth, or some combination. They each serve useful purposes, so don't assume that you can't get letters of recommendation just because you aren't an A-student. And don't assume that just being an A-student will get you much of a recommendation. The most helpful recommendations combine academic and personal assessment. The surly, difficult A-student is not necessarily more desirable than the eager, hardworking, promising B- or C-student. (Don't even think about being a surly, difficult student—unless you are so talented and brilliant that the rest of us will be forced to overlook your unpleasantness. And if you are *brilliant*, why not be grateful and gracious?)

• **Demonstrate good character and motivation.** Show up for all classes, and be on time for class. Turn in assignments on time and in proper format.

• **Show that you learn from criticism.** If weaknesses are identified in essays or papers, make sure not to repeat them in subsequent work.

• **Take more than one class from the same professor.** It is much easier to write recommendations for students we know something about. Taking additional courses from the same instructor increases the chances that the instructor will be able to write a strong letter on your behalf. Some instructors will feel uncomfortable writing a letter of recommendation for a student who has only taken one class with them, no matter how well you do in that one class. The exception is classes that involve regular discussion, lots of writing, and office visits. In those circumstances, most instructors will be able to write effective letters of recommendation for good students.

• **Request your letter in a timely fashion.** Ask for your letter at least two weeks before you need it.

• **Politely check on your letter's progress in one week.**

• **Provide *pertinent written information* when you make your request.** It's a very good idea to provide a *written statement* of your plans and goals at the time you ask for a letter of recommendation. Also mention any helpful personal information: Are you a parent? Do you work? Where? How many hours? What's your major? What's your immediate goal (scholarship, four-year transfer, graduate school, and so on)? What's your long-term goal (psychologist, philosopher, preacher, engineer, nurse, forest ranger)?

• **Provide a copy of your transcript and a list of your current courses when you request a letter of recommendation.** Be sure to flag any courses you've taken from the instructor you're asking to write the letter.

• **Choose your letter writers wisely.** Select instructors who know your abilities and can honestly recommend you with enthusiasm. In today's world of inflated recommendations, a mediocre letter can be worse than no letter.

• **Always *ask* if the professor can comfortably write a strong letter for you.** Too often, today's letters of recommendation are grossly inflated. As embarrassing and disappointing as it can be to learn that your professor doesn't feel that she can write you a strong recommendation, it's much better to learn that before a weak letter has done its damage.

• **Be sure to get some letters from instructors in courses that are relevant to your future plans.** A letter from your philosophy instructor is not likely to carry as much weight for admissions to a music program as one from your music theory instructor. Failure to provide relevant letters may arouse concern in those reviewing your application.

• **If your instructors give you copies of their letters, keep them together in a file—and keep a backup file in a separate safe place.** This is good advice even if you are registered with the school's placement service.

• **Don't leave college without at least three letters of recommendation.** Just because you don't plan to continue in school doesn't mean you won't need letters of recommendation. People change their minds. Further, good college recommendations can be used when applying for jobs, admission to police or firefighting academies, and special military programs. Potential employers will look for signs of responsibility, ambition, maturity, ability to solve problems, complete a program, and so forth.

• **Don't forget to set up a dossier file at your school's placement office.**

CHAPTER 8

Test Taking

Before the gates of excellence, the high gods have placed sweat.
Hesiod

Though it may not always seem like it, tests are designed to see what you have learned in a particular course, not what you don't know. Fortunately, there are basic guidelines for maximizing your chances of doing well on any kind of test. This section covers basic test preparation and specific tips for essay, short-answer, and objective tests.

PREPARING FOR TESTS

- **STUDY, STUDY, STUDY.** The single best preparation for any kind of test is practicing effective study habits on a routine basis.

- **Take advantage of "free" tests and quizzes.** If your instructor offers extra-credit tests, or drops one or more tests, be sure to take every test. Dropped or extra-credit tests amount to free practice.

- **Be sure to attend any test reviews.** Some instructors devote the class period preceding a test to last-minute questions and review.

Be sure to take advantage of such an opportunity by coming to class with written questions.

• **Study as if all tests are essay tests, whether they are or not.** Studies have shown that students perform worse when they gear their studying to objective tests. In one experiment, one group of students was told to prepare for an essay test, but actually given an objective test. Another group of students was told to prepare for, and actually given, an objective test. The students who had been expecting an essay test did markedly better. This pattern has been confirmed many times. (See below for specific advice on studying for essay tests.)

• **Avoid cramming.** Although some students insist that they learn best under pressure, research suggests caution. Too much anxiety interferes with critical thinking skills and other cognitive abilities. Memory retention markedly declines, the ability to reason diminishes, even perceptual skill decreases under extreme anxiety and stress. Also, skills classes require regular practice. Courses such as logic, critical thinking, most science, and all math courses cover both information and skills, so cramming cannot compensate for regular, incremental studying.

• **Get your normal amount of sleep the night before the test.** Fatigue produces and exacerbates some of the same conditions as anxiety: impaired retention of information, "processing errors" (misreading, spelling mistakes, filling in the wrong part of the exam, overlooking key instructions), and diminished thinking skills. Sleep deprivation can also trigger depression and other "down" emotions which interfere with testing well.

• **Study under conditions similar to actual testing conditions.** For example, avoid drinking caffeinated drinks while you study unless you are sure you can drink them during or right before the exam. Studies show that students have a much higher rate of retrieving information when their biochemical state is the same as when they learned it: students who sipped coffee while studying did better on tests when they were allowed to sip coffee during the test than when they weren't.

• **Eat wisely before the test.** Don't eat a big meal or candy bar right before the test. The last thing you want to experience during a test is that drowsy feeling that can follow a big meal. But do eat and drink lightly before the test. When your blood sugar is too low during a test, you can feel shaky, weak, and confused. You can also be confused if you're severely dehydrated.

• **Allow extra time to get to class on test day.** Again, do all that you can to avoid disruptive anxiety. Get to class early enough to select your usual seat; make sure you have any necessary pens, pencils, paper, bluebooks, notes (if allowed).

> **VERY IMPORTANT TIP:** Always pick up your graded test and attend class the day the test is discussed. Your grade is not the only thing that matters. Learning from mistakes and correcting errors will pay off on subsequent tests. Collecting and studying each and every test is the first step in preparing for your next test.

RELAXATION TECHNIQUES FOR BETTER TEST SCORES

Practice the following relaxation techniques—especially if you tend to panic on tests:

• **Stretch slowly and leisurely before taking your seat.**

• **Remind yourself that your performance on the test, no matter how important, does not measure your worth as a human being, or predict your chances of finding ultimate happiness.**

• **Remind yourself that you are already a test-taking expert.** You've already taken hundreds, if not thousands of tests, in grade school and high school, perhaps in the military or applying for jobs.

• **Take a tip from successful athletes and performers:** *visualize yourself taking the test and doing well.* *Creative visualization* is not the same thing as vaguely imagining something. Visualization is not a dreamy fantasy, but a detailed, focused, highly concentrated, carefully structured, step-by-step mental imaging of a future event; in this case, the test. Sports and performance psychologists report that creative visualization can enhance the effectiveness of *prepared and capable* athletes and performers in a variety of fields. Visualization is not a substitute for solid preparation.

• **Practice deep breathing.** Force yourself to breathe deeply and slowly, especially when you are nervous and your natural inclination is to hyperventilate.

• **Immediately after you receive the test, put your pencil down, put the test facedown, close your eyes, place both hands on the desk, and breathe slowly and deeply for a few seconds.** Tell yourself that you will do well. These few seconds can save you from rushing into the test in a state of unproductive anxiety.

• **Then:** *Slowly* **turn your test over,** *slowly* **read it through,** *slowly* **pick up your pencil, and go to work.** Consciously avoid the kind of jerky, "hyper" movements associated with panic or fear. Such movements actually reinforce and stimulate panic or fear. Monitor your breathing, too. When you feel panicked, put your pencil down and practice deep breathing for a few seconds.

• **Be thankful for a** *touch of anxiety.* Clinical studies have shown that a bit of anxiety can be an advantage because moderately heightened adrenal function (short of a panic level) *increases cognitive and perceptual acuity.* Some anxiety is normal and usually helpful.

> Deal with it before it is there; check disorder before it is rife. Deal with the hard while it is still easy, the great while it is still small.
>
> *Laotse*

HOW TO DO YOUR BEST ON ESSAY TESTS

- *Read* the whole test *before answering any questions.*

- **Follow all instructions.** Note the time limit, if any. Note if you must answer all questions or only some. Pay attention to the relative value of questions.

- **Familiarize yourself with *all* questions before answering *any*.** This will allow you to organize a strategy for getting the most correct answers. Further, the answer to one question may remind you of the answer to another.

- **First answer the questions you know the most about.** Don't worry if these questions aren't worth as much as other questions. Beginning from strength has a number of advantages: You can get right to work, thus maximizing your time. You're sure to have some correct answers. You'll boost your confidence and reduce anxiety. You'll kick your mind into gear quickly, and avoid the panic and confusion that can result from wrestling with a question that draws a blank.

- **When in doubt, write.** If you can't think of anything to write about any question, write something about one of them anyway. On scratch paper preferably (if scratch paper is allowed), write down anything you can remember that's even remotely connected to the question. If you keep writing, you'll probably discover information, connections, and patterns that seemed beyond reach. You may have to scrap most of this "creative" writing once your mind kicks into gear, and write a more polished essay, but that's all right.

- **Neatness counts**. Your instructor should not have to decipher bad handwriting or decode crossed-out passages, or convoluted arrows connecting a sentence on page two to one on page four. If you must make extensive corrections to an essay answer, completely and clearly cross out the undesired work. Ask the instructor or proctor if you can begin on a new sheet of paper, if necessary.

- **If you are responsible for providing your own bluebooks or paper, be sure to have plenty of the kind specified.** Some instructors require their students to bring in bluebooks a class period or two before the test. They then check to insure that the bluebooks are blank, and may stamp or sign them to indicate this. Allow ample time to buy your bluebooks and take extra precautions not to fold or wrinkle them. Your instructor may refuse to grade a test written on unapproved paper or in an unapproved bluebook.

• **Never use your own paper without asking, and don't go fishing around through your notebook or book bag for paper or pens, or anything else.** You might know you're not cheating, but your instructor may not.

• **Use complete sentences; don't use abbreviations unless explicitly informed that you may; use good grammar.** Essay tests ask for *essays*, not collections of fragmentary notes. Bad grammar is almost always associated with cloudy thinking. At the very least, bad grammar weakens your ideas.

• **Spell all technical terms and proper names correctly.** There is absolutely no excuse for not learning how to spell the important terms that are introduced as part of a course. This applies to terms derived from Greek, Latin, and other languages that are difficult for you. The fact that a word is unusual or hard to pronounce just means that you have to work a little harder to become comfortable with it.

• **Mention specific relevant examples, persons, titles, and so forth from assigned readings, the textbook, and the instructor's lectures.** Be specific. Show that you are knowledgeable in terms of *this class*. Essay tests have two functions: to show that you can think on a sophisticated level *and* to show that you have acquired new information. Your essays should always present information in a coherent fashion.

• **Make and *show* connections; don't just list facts and information.** Avoid the extremes of the overly general essay that does not reveal an adequate fund of information, and the "pseudo-essay" that is so crammed with facts that it is not a coherent essay at all.

- **Make sure to answer the question that is asked.** Pay attention to such instructions as "compare and contrast," "explain why," "analyze," and so forth. Follow instructions. Your instructor may not give credit for wonderful insights, no matter how brilliantly expressed, if they are not responsive to the question *as it is framed*.

- **Don't combine questions.** Even if the answers to two or three questions overlap, it's best to answer each question separately and exactly as it asked. Grading essays is hard work, and most instructors will find evaluating combined essays especially difficult, because even related questions call for different emphasis.

- **Keep track of the time.** Don't try to write perfect essays. You might spend too much time on one or two questions. Allow time for a quick scan of all your answers at the end of the testing period so you can catch any glaring errors or omissions.

- **Answer *every* required question.** Partial credit (no matter how little) is far better than no credit. Your instructor has good reasons for the combination of questions included on your test, so don't defeat them by avoiding the required questions. Every once in a while I have a student answer extra optional questions to "compensate" for not answering one or more required questions. This never works. It's like having a mechanic adjust your brakes when you have a steering problem—because he's not able to fix the steering.

- **Reread your answer before turning it in.** Consider proofreading your answer as a vital part of writing it. It may be tempting (and common) to write up to the last second, but it is more effective not to have to. This is another reason to be very well prepared for the test: you will be able to start writing right away, and will have many valuable things to say.

- **Write a clear conclusion/summation that uses key phrases and examples from your essay (just as you would for an out-of-class assignment).** Psychologically, a lucid, focused conclusion encourages your reader to look more favorably on your essay than just stopping in the middle of

- **Be sure you have put your name on your test.**

HOW TO DO YOUR BEST ON COMPLETION TESTS

- **Read the entire test before answering any questions.** Later questions may contain useful information for answering earlier questions, and vice versa. Reading the entire test gives you the "lay of the land," so you can maximize your time by first going quickly through questions you know very well, and then concentrating on more complex or difficult questions.

- **Follow instructions.** This is always important, but it is crucial when tests are scored by teaching assistants or student aides who may not have the expertise or authority to deal with improvisations or modifications of the requested format.

- **Use the kind of pen or pencil required, and be very careful when you fill in your answers or erase them.** It is difficult and tiring to read light, brightly colored inks and very light (hard) pencil lead. You should always use black or blue ink or a No. 2 pencil, unless your instructor specifies otherwise.

- **Spell technical terms and proper names correctly. Do not abbreviate.** *Always* assume spelling counts.

- **Write legibly.**

- **Confine your answers to the space allowed.** If you are allowed to use additional space, mark your continuations very clearly. But always ask before assuming you can use additional space.

- **Pay attention to key words and phrases; underline them *if you're allowed to.*** Key words include qualifiers like: always, never, usually, mostly, sometimes, not, in part, without exception. Watch for important qualifiers like "according to the text," or "in lecture."

- **Answer every question.** In most cases, you will be graded on the number of correct answers (check to be sure). An empty blank and a wrong answer are both worth zero. You have nothing to lose by writing something (and you may be correct and not know it). You might get partial credit.

• **Don't waste time dwelling on difficult questions.** Keep going, and come back to difficult questions after you've made one complete pass through the test.

• **Review the test before you turn it in.** The review process does more than catch omissions and errors, it can also trigger answers that were just out of reach before.

• **Don't forget to put your name on your test.**

HOW TO DO YOUR BEST ON OBJECTIVE TESTS

• **Read the entire test before answering any questions.** Later questions may contain useful information for answering earlier questions, and vice versa. Reading the entire test gives you the "lay of the land," so you can maximize your time by first going quickly through questions you know very well, and then concentrating on more complex or difficult questions.

• **Follow instructions.** This is always important, but it is crucial when tests are machine scored.

• **If your test will be machine scored, use the kind of pen or pencil required, and be very careful when you fill in your answers or erase them.** The most common grading machines are made to read clearly defined, heavy black pencil markings. The safest kind of pencil to use is the "No. 2" type. No. 2 grade lead is soft enough to make a dark mark, but hard enough not to smudge. Some machines require special pencils.

• **If you are responsible for providing your own machine-scored answer sheets, be sure to bring two or three forms of the kind specified.** Allow ample time to buy your answer sheets, and take extra precautions not to fold or wrinkle them. Your instructor may refuse to grade an answer sheet that cannot be read by the grading machine.

- **Answer the easiest questions first.** You want to score as many correct answers as quickly as possible. Also, the positive experience of providing correct answers will boost your confidence, minimize test anxiety, and probably help you recall the answers to at least some of the questions that you passed over so far.

- **If all questions are of equal weight, don't dawdle over difficult questions until you have made one complete pass through the test.**

- **Pay attention to key words and phrases; underline them** *if you're allowed to.* Key words include qualifiers like: always, never, usually, mostly, sometimes, not, in part, without exception. Watch for important qualifiers like "according to the text," or "in lecture."

- **On true-false questions, pay special attention to universal terms like "always," "all," and "never."** Such terms allow for no exceptions. If you're not sure of the answer to a question containing universal qualifiers, your best guess is false.

- **On multiple-choice questions, mentally turn each choice into a true-false question.** The leading statement plus the correct choice always yields a true statement (assuming only one correct answer). After you've chosen an answer, read the leading statement plus your choice to see if they produce a true statement. Here's a simple example:

> 10. Plato was the pupil of _____ and the teacher of _____.
> A. Aristotle, Socrates
> B. Diogenes, Socrates
> C. Socrates, Aristotle
> D. Aristotle, Alexander the Great
> E. None of these.

The correct answer is C. If we add C to the leading statement, we get: "Plato was the pupil of *Socrates* and the teacher of *Aristotle*." This is a true statement. No other choice produces a true statement when added to the leading statement.

• **On multiple-choice questions, always choose the most precise correct answer if more than one choice is correct.** If you are expected to select the "best" option on multiple-choice questions, it helps to think of selecting one option as *rejecting the other options*. Here's an example from a logic test to help illustrate this point. In this class, an argument was defined as *a group of propositions, one of which (the conclusion) is claimed to follow logically from other propositions (premises)*. Which answer would you select as the "best" answer based on the italicized definition?

> 28. An argument consists of _____ .
>   A. a group of propositions
>   B. at least one premise
>   C. a conclusion
>   D. A, B, and C
>   E. None of these.

Congratulations if you picked D; it's the "best" answer. A, B, and C are each "correct" in the sense that an argument does contain a group of propositions (A), one of which is the conclusion (C), and at least one of which is a premise (B). The problem with picking A, B, or C is a function of the nature of multiple-choice questions: *picking the one best multiple-choice option has the effect of denying all of the other options*. This can be easily illustrated by analyzing exactly what's involved with picking option A. Picking option A amounts to saying this: "An argument consists of a group of propositions, but *not* at least one premise and *not* a conclusion." Picking B amounts to saying: "An argument consists of at least one premise, but *not* a group of propositions and *not* a conclusion." Picking C amounts to saying: "An argument consists of a conclusion, but *not* a group of propositions and *not* at least one premise." Picking E is the worst possible answer.

• **Do not look for patterns among the answers; answer each question independently.** Don't worry, for example, about how many "true's" or how many "C's" there are. It is quite possible that by accident or diabolical instructor scheming all the answers are true or C—or no answer is C, or true, and so forth.

• **Answer each question exactly as it is worded; don't "mentally correct" or rewrite it.** It is unfortunately quite common for test takers to ignore key words or phrases in questions, or to "mentally correct" them.

Here's an example of mentally "correcting" a question: I once assigned a random ID number to students to use in posting grades. The first day syllabus stated, "You must put your random ID number on all tests, once you have been assigned a number. NO ASSIGNMENTS WILL BE GRADED WITHOUT THIS NUMBER." The second week of class I gave a test over the course syllabus. I had not yet assigned random numbers. One of the true-false questions was "You must put your random ID number on all tests." Every student picked true. The correct answer was false. To be true the statement would have to be amended as follows: "You must put your random ID number on all tests, *once you have been assigned a number.*"

The class accused me of being "nit picky" and unfair. I pointed out that the statement was obviously false *since no one was required to use a random number on this very test!* I explained that since this was a test for which a random number was not required, the statement "You must put your random ID number on *all* tests" had to be false. Quite a few students said something like this: "I figured you didn't mean this test. I figured you *meant* once we have our numbers. . . ." In other words, those students modified the wording of the question; they mentally altered it according to their own ideas of how it should read.

• **Don't mentally *add* or *delete* phrases to questions.** (See the preceding discussion.) You might do this without being aware of it. Next time you're going over a corrected test, be alert for this tendency. See if you are somehow altering the questions from their actual wording.

• **If a question seems utterly unintelligible or lacking any correct answer, ask your instructor for clarification.** The worst that can happen is that you're told that the question is correct. Then you can rethink it or go on to questions you can answer. But you might be right. Tests sometimes do contain errors.

•   **Change answers only if you have good reasons.** Statistically, more students change from correct answers to incorrect ones, than from incorrect to correct ones. But not always. So think twice if you find yourself tempted to change lots of answers, but don't be afraid to change an answer if you have a good reason to.

•   **Double check your answer sheet before turning it in.** Make sure you've used the proper kind of pen or pencil and erased cleanly. Count your answers and check to see if you've skipped a line or put two answers on one line.

•   **Be sure your name is on your answer sheet (and your test, if required).**

HOW TO DO YOUR BEST
ON MIXED-QUESTION TESTS

•   **On tests containing more than one kind of question, first scan the entire test, and then answer questions in this order: multiple-choice first, true-false second, completion third, and essay last—regardless of the order in which they occur on your test.** As a rule, you can improve your test scores by following this order. Multiple-choice questions provide a selective review of material, without requiring the cold recollection of completion questions or the tantalizing seductiveness of true-false questions. Multiple-choice questions provide information and trigger recall for the prepared student. Answering specific, objective, questions first reinforces basic information about the material.

•   **Take your time, but don't dawdle; you'll want to allow time to reread and change answers.**

•   **Don't dwell on questions that are not worth very many points.** *Having read the entire test before answering any questions* helps you budget your time according to the relative weight of each section.

• **Be sure you understand the rules for matching-type questions.** Can the same choice be used to match more than one item? Must every choice be used? Be very clear on these conditions. If they are not stated on the test, ask your instructor.

• **As always, be sure to reread your answers before turning in your test.**

• **Remember: Your best bet is to study as if all tests are essay tests.**

• **Review the previous material pertaining to specific kinds of tests.**

• **Be sure your name is on your test.**

CONCLUSION

How long do you put off thinking yourself worthy of the best things . . . what sort of teacher are you still waiting for, that you put off improving yourself until he comes? You are not a [child] anymore, but already . . . full grown.

Epictetus

If you've learned anything from this book, I hope it's that you have a great deal of influence over your grade in philosophy, and your entire college experience. The tips and advice in *How to Get the Most Out of Philosophy* can help you avoid certain pitfalls and increase your chances of success—but they cannot provide you with the will and drive necessary to succeed.

The *wish* to do well is common. The *will* and *sustained drive* to do what's necessary to do well are less common. Regardless of your past performance in school, and regardless of your "native ability," you can take deliberate, time-tested steps to improve your chances of learning philosophy and getting a good grade in the process. There are no substitutes for regular, organized *work*, however.

You probably won't be able (or want) to follow every suggestion in this book. That's to be expected. Try out a few ideas that seem most helpful given your current strengths and weaknesses. Wisdom teaches that though we cannot do everything, we can always do something.

Decide right now that you want a full, rich *education*, the kind of education that goes beyond merely getting a job and degree (as important as they may be). Getting a degree is not the same thing as getting an education. All around us we see "college educated" experts dumping garbage into our waterways, robbing people of their pensions, or just being dissatisfied and unhappy. Sadly, *not every college graduate is well educated.*

You will discover that when your focus shifts from just getting a grade and a degree to developing skills and learning to appreciate things of substance, your whole attitude becomes more receptive to learning. Grades do count, but they're not all that counts.

It's easy to forget that this is *your* education. Customize it. Work at it. *By enrolling in college, you are accepting a personal invitation to participate in "the great conversation."* Socrates guided others out of the cave of ignorance, but they provided the effort. I hope this "map" helps you on your way "out of the cave." The next steps are up you.

> Say not, "When I have leisure I will study." Perhaps you will have no leisure. *Hillel*

BEGINNING PHILOSOPHER'S
BIBLIOGRAPHY

There is no such thing as an interesting book, there are only interested readers.

Ralph Waldo Emerson

Following is a list of books about writing, thinking, and succeeding in college. I have included focused, brief books that can be read quickly or studied on an as-needed basis, if you wish to supplement the material in this book.

PHILOSOPHICALLY-ORIENTED STUDY BOOKS

Sylvan Barnet and Hugo Bedau, editors. *Critical Thinking, Reading, and Writing: A Brief Guide to Argument.* Boston: Bedford Books of St. Martin's Press, 1993. This 230-page book includes a good chapter on sources and documentation.

Zachary Seech. *Writing Philosophy Papers.* Belmont, Ca.: Wadsworth Publishing Company, 1993. An excellent guide to writing philosophy papers, this 134-page text is not only valuable to philosophy students; its contents can be applied to any critical writing assignments.

Mark B. Woodhouse. *A Preface to Philosophy*, Fifth Edition. Belmont, Ca.: Wadsworth Publishing Company, 1994. This 174-page survey of what philosophy is all about includes a handy glossary of philosophical terms.

PHILOSOPHY REFERENCE BOOKS

Peter A. Angeles. *Dictionary of Philosophy*. New York: Barnes & Noble Books, 1981.

Simon Blackburn. *The Oxford Dictionary of Philosophy*. Oxford: Oxford University Press, 1994. This witty, up-to-date and authoritative philosophical dictionary includes useful cross-references.

The Blackwell Companion to Philosophy. Nicholas Bunnin and E. P. Tsui-James, editors. Oxford: Blackwell Publishers Ltd., 1996. Although presented as a textbook, this is an excellent reference book for the serious philosopher: technical, thorough, and carefully edited.

A Companion to Ethics. Peter Singer, editor. Oxford: Blackwell Publishers Ltd., 1993. This solid addition to the Blackwell Companion to Philosophy series consists of 47 entries written by some of today's leading philosophers; entries include up-to-date bibliographies.

The Oxford Companion to Philosophy. Ted Honderich, editor. Oxford: Oxford University Press, 1995. Checking in at a massive 1009 pages, Honderich's text is one of the most thorough single-volume reference books available—nearly an encyclopedia.

Frederick Copleston, S.J. *A History of Philosophy*. New York: Doubleday, Image edition, 1985. Copleston's strength is his ability to summarize and explain other philosophers' ideas without intruding. His own editorial comments are always clearly identified. An excellent history, now available in a cumbersome, but affordable, three-book edition. The individual nine-volume series is still available in most large bookstores; these smaller books are much easier to handle.

A Dictionary of Philosophy. Thomas Mautner, editor. Oxford: Blackwell Publishers Ltd., 1996. This dictionary contains entries from more than one hundred distinguished philosophers.

The Encyclopedia of Philosophy. Paul Edwards, editor. New York: Macmillan & Free Press, 1967. Two versions of this indispensable source are available, the regular edition of eight separate volumes and a four-volume "student edition" that contains exactly the same material. Though some of the articles in the Encyclopedia can be difficult for novice philosophers, this is an excellent source of general information regarding philosophers and philosophical issues and arguments.

Ben-Ami Scharfstein. *The Philosophers: Their Lives and the Nature of Their Thought*. Oxford: Oxford University Press, 1989. Scharfstein's little book is a fascinating blend of philosophy, history, and psychology.

GENERAL STUDY SKILLS

William H. Armstrong. *Study Is Hard Work*, Second Edition. Boston: David R. Godine, 1995. Run to your nearest library or bookstore and grab a copy of this 148-page classic by the author of *Sounder*. Among other things (writing and herding sheep, to mention two), Armstrong taught history for over fifty years. His wise, honest book is sobering and inspiring in that best of ways: It calls on the best in us.

James Deese and Ellin K. Deese. *How to Study*, Third Edition Revised. New York: McGraw-Hill Book Company, 1979. Don't be fooled by the copyright date. This 120-page primer concentrates on reading. A minor classic.

Ron Fry. *"Ace" any Test*. Hawthorne, N.J.: Career Press, 1992. I found this to be a zippy, witty, practical 96-page handbook.

J. J. Gibbs. *Dancing With Your Books: The Zen Way of Studying*. New York: Penguin Books, 1990. This 181-page surprise is elegant and soothing, a book worth keeping.

Marvin Lunenfeld and Peter Lunenfeld. *College Basics: How to Start Right and Finish Strong*. Buffalo, N. Y.: Semester Press,

1991. This 144-page college self-help book, written by a father and his son who are also a professor and a student, packs a lot of useful material into a modest size.

Virginia Voeks. *On Becoming an Educated Person: An Orientation to College and Life.* Philadelphia: Saunders College Publishing, 1979. This is an excellent, wise, and substantial (248 pages) book that really lives up to its title.

Richard Watson. *Good Teaching: A Guide for Students.* Carbondale and Edwardsville, Il.: Southern Illinois University Press, 1997. Watson is a wonderful writer: Acerbic, profound, and dead-on honest. This 48-page volume pulls no punches in its charge to students: You are responsible for learning. Watson writes from the unique perspective of being a respected scholar and teacher at a first-rate research university. It's a wise student who listens to advice from "insiders," and Richard Watson is tough, caring, and funny.

SPECIALIZED SUBJECTS

Stephen S. Carey. *A Beginner's Guide to Scientific Method.* Belmont, Ca.: Wadsworth Publishing Company, 1994. This clearly written, 124-page book helps students master the critical thinking skills that are specific to science through the use of entertaining and worthwhile exercises.

Roseann Giarrusso, Judith Richlin-Klonsky, William G. Roy, and Ellen Strenski. *A Guide to Writing Sociology Papers*, Third Edition. New York: St. Martin's Press, 1994. This 180-page text includes writing samples and strategies.

Richard Manning Smith. *Mastering Mathematics: How to be a Great Math Student*, Second Edition. Belmont, Ca.: Wadsworth Publishing Company, 1994. At 198 pages, this is one of the most effective how-to books on the market.

SEVEN GUIDES TO BETTER WRITING

Philosophy instructors tend to accept any consistent "commonly used" system of citations. The Chicago (Turabian) and MLA style guides are the most commonly used formats for most subject areas. *The Blair Handbook* is a comprehensive (910 pages) guide to the entire writing process. Psychology students may be required to use the APA style for term papers and essays.

Chicago Manual of Style, 14th Edition. John Grossman and Alice Bennett, editors. Chicago: University of Chicago Press, 1993.

Toby Fulwer, and Alan R. Hayakawa. *The Blair Handbook*. Englewood Cliffs, N. J.: Prentice Hall, 1994.

Joseph Gibaldi. *MLA Handbook for Writers of Research Papers*, Fourth Edition. New York: Modern Language Association, 1995.

Muriel Harris. Prentice Hall Reference Guide to Grammar and Usage, Second Edition. Englewood Cliffs, N.J.: Prentice Hall, 1994.

Publication Manual of the American Psychological Association, Third Edition. Washington, D. C.: American Psychological Association, 1983.

William Strunk, Jr., and E. B. White. *Elements of Style*, Third Edition. New York: Macmillan, 1979.

Kate L. Turabian. *A Manual for Writers of Term Papers, Theses, and Dissertations*, Sixth Edition. Revised by John Grossman and Alice Bennett. Chicago: University of Chicago Press, 1996.

PHILOSOPHY ONLINE

Many college and university philosophy departments have websites. You can get information about them through institutional homepages. Here are some particularly interesting online philosophy sites for you to check out.

American Philosophical Association. The APA is the major professional organization for American philosophers. You can check out all sorts of information about meetings held by various philosophical groups, e-mail addresses for philosophers, university homepages, and such. The APA's home on the World Wide Web is: **www.udel.edu/apa.** Questions and comments are welcome at: **apaOnline@udel.edu**

Episteme Links. This commercial website provides links to electronic texts, journals, papers, philosophers, pictures of philosophers, and a humor section. *Episteme Links* can be found at: **www.arrowweb.com./philo**

Ethics Updates. Professor Lawrence M. Hinman, of the University of San Diego, has established a website that presents a forum covering various categories of ethics education. *Ethics Updates* can be found at: **www.acusd.edu/ethics**

Philosophy Documentation Center. The Philosophy Documentation is an electronic archive and publishing house that contains an electronic database of articles by professional philosophers, electronic journals, and *Books in Philosophy*, which is the world's largest mail-order supplier of philosophy books. The PDC also publishes tutorial software for logic. The PDC e-mail address is: **kswope@bgnet.bgsu.edu**   The PDC website is at: **http://www.bgsu.edu/pdc/**

Wadsworth Philosophy Shop. The publisher of this book has a nifty website with all sorts of information about their philosophy publications (as you might expect). This website contains much more than that, however. It is a great opportunity to browse in a specialized "virtual bookstore," and to communicate with active philosophers from around the world. The Wadsworth Philosophy Shop can be found at: **http://philosophy.wadsworth.com**

Zeno's Coffeehouse. Valdosta State University philosopher professor Ron Barnette says that his creation is "Designed to make philosophy, and a spot for philosophical reflection and relaxation, accessible to a wide Internet audience. " Check it out at: **http://www.valdosta.peachnet.edu/~rbarnett/phi/zeno.html**